◄ WILLIAM CLOUD AND ROBERT GRANFIELD ►

Recovery from Addiction

A PRACTICAL GUIDE TO TREATMENT, SELF-HELP, AND QUITTING ON YOUR OWN

NEW YORK UNIVERSITY PRESS

New York and London

NEW YORK UNIVERSITY PRESS
New York and London

Library of Congress Cataloging-in-Publication Data
Cloud, William, 1947–
Recovery from addiction : a practical guide to treatment, self-help,
and quitting on your own / William Cloud and Robert Granfield.
p. cm.
ISBN 0-8147-1607-5 (alk. paper) —
ISBN 0-8147-1608-3 (pbk. : alk. paper)
1. Substance abuse—Treatment. 2. Addicts—Rehabilitation.
3. Self-help techniques. I. Granfield, Robert, 1955– II. Title.
HV4998 .C56 2001
362.29'18—dc21   00-012880

New York University Press books are printed on acid-free paper,
and their binding materials are chosen for strength and durability.

Manufactured in the United States of America

10 9 8 7 6 5 4 3 2 1

For Willie Mae Whatley

◀ CONTENTS ▶

◄ ACKNOWLEDGMENTS ►

This book is a tribute to those whose lives have touched ours through our practice, research, teaching, and training over the course of our more than fifty collective years of work in the area of substance abuse. We are fortunate to have learned so much from those who have personally suffered from addiction and from those studying to become practitioners to provide help to them. The heroic stories of our study participants and the insightful comments about our work from our students, at the baccalaureate, master's, and doctoral levels, compelled us to put the content of this book on the printed page. We would especially like to thank Pat Fitzpatrick, Mike Carter, Lynne Lehrner, and Jim Vanos for their contributions to this project. We would also like to acknowledge the helpful comments of those who have participated or continue to participate in Alcohol Anonymous and other 12-step groups. Their observations were especially relevant to the subject matter of this book. We also thank Jennifer Hammer, our editor at New York University Press, for her dedicated interest in our work. Finally, we would like to acknowledge the enduring support of our families, as they sacrificed many family activities during the summer of 2000 so that we could meet our targeted writing deadline—thanks, Karen, Allison, and Marian for your loving patience.

CHAPTER 1

Introduction

Each year several million people choose, or are encouraged by loved ones, to enter treatment or join self-help groups for their alcohol and/or drug-related problems. Not unlike first-time consumers of other services, consumers of treatment and those who care about them are generally uninformed about these services and unfamiliar with the range of possible treatment options and types of self-help groups currently available. They are also likely to be unaware of why a particular approach would be a good choice for one kind of problem but a poor choice or even harmful for another. In the understandable state of urgency that many people who experience drug problems confront, they and their loved ones may rush to the first treatment option they encounter. Yet some approaches to resolving addiction are inappropriate for certain types of situations or simply do not work. More importantly, how you attempt to resolve your substance abuse problems can have profound and lifelong consequences. This guide is meant to introduce you to the range of recovery options available so that you can choose the approach that is best for you.

Consumers of treatment services tend to be unaware of many of the emerging controversies surrounding alcohol and drug treatment. Experts disagree about fundamental questions concerning what actually causes addiction to alcohol and other drugs and how best to treat it. Consumers are also unlikely to be aware of the range of criticisms currently leveled at traditional treatment approaches by an increasing number of researchers.

Over the last few decades, addiction has commonly come to be perceived as a lifelong disease that will continue to get worse unless interrupted by treatment. However, much recent research challenges this narrow biological explanation of addiction as a "disease" and the necessity to treat all cases of substance dependency.

The mistaken belief that treatment is always necessary in overcoming addiction comes from putting too much stock in biological explanations of substance dependency and underestimating the role of other critical psychological, social, and environmental factors. By viewing drug-dependent persons as sufferers of a disease, this approach has inadvertently resulted in a number of addiction remedies that ignore the social circumstances that can play a pivotal role when it comes to the use and abuse of substances.

There is no medical cure for addiction, no magic pill, and

no surgical procedure to remove addiction from the body. This is because addiction has less to do with physical reality and much more to do with social and psychological experiences. People overcome addictions when they come to view their excessive use of intoxicants as deleterious and when they experience improvements in their lives in relation to work, family, community, and the many enriching relationships that develop as a result.

People often ask us how to identify and select the most appropriate treatment for their problem and what are the advantages and disadvantages of treatment and self-help groups. They also ask how they should go about attempting to resolve their addiction without treatment. Here we attempt to address these questions.

This book is a consumer's guide to treatment, self-help, and natural recovery for users, family members, students, and practitioners. We provide you with detailed information about the various approaches to recovery in order to illuminate the options available to people with alcohol and drug addictions as they contemplate their own recovery paths. In order to make this book accessible to a large audience, we have purposely resisted the temptation to provide citations from our own research and the research of other experts. For those who wish to examine the available data and research, particularly as it relates to self-resolution from addiction, readers are advised to review our earlier book, *Coming Clean: Overcoming Addiction without Treatment*, which will provide you with over six hundred academic citations we use to support our research.

As a potential consumer of these services, you are provided with information about these programs so that you will be able to make the choice that is best for you. Our presentation is broad in scope. We do not offer details on all the possible treatment and self-help options available to you; rather, our purpose is to present general descriptions and insights that will provide you with a framework for making informed decisions about these options. Let us point out, however, that in providing information about treatment and self-help groups, we are in no way advocating any particular therapeutic or self-help option. If we advocate anything, it is this: most people overcome addictions to alcohol and drugs without treatment, and, therefore, as people contemplate their own recoveries, they might first consider attempting a natural recovery. We detail how to go about the natural recovery process in Part Two of this book. However, we recognize that for a variety of reasons, a person confronting a drug addiction may feel more comfortable seeking out formal treatment or may be in the unfortunate position of having treatment imposed upon him or her by others. So, while we advocate that individuals who are struggling to overcome their addictions consider natural recovery options, we provide information on treatment and self-help for those who are, for one or assorted reasons, unable or uninterested in adopting this pathway to overcome addiction.

Our purpose in writing this book stems from a genuine interest in helping people overcome the problems they are experiencing through their use of alcohol and drugs. As you will see, we do not believe that recovery is contingent upon treatment, we do not believe that recovery is contingent upon abstinence, and, perhaps most importantly, we do not believe that addiction is a disease. We offer information and ideas that will hopefully allow you to reflect on your use and assist you in finding your own road away from addiction.

We would like to add one final caveat about the language that we adopt throughout this book. We are keenly aware of the power of language to create meaning, to distort, and to perpetuate unfounded images of reality. The language that is used to discuss and describe the world of alcohol and drug problems is particularly problematic and often overly moralistic. However, in order to communicate with one another, we are sometimes forced into using language that might not be sufficient to describe more subtle understandings of the world. Such is the case in this book. In our use of terms such as "addiction" and "recovery," we do not affix any essential or biological characteristic to the described behavior. For instance, when we use the term "addiction," we in no way mean to suggest that this behavior is a disease or that individuals who are addicted will be so permanently. Similarly, when we discuss recovery, we do not mean to convey the idea of recovery in a medical sense of having an illness, but rather we use it to refer to the behavioral cessation of the habitual and often damaging use of intoxicating substances. While many people in treatment or in self-help groups see themselves as "in recovery," those who have recovered without treatment most often see themselves as having "recovered." Some of these self-remitters even purposely choose not to employ the language of "recovery" and, in doing so, reject the premise that they have, or once had, a disease.

Drawing on our combined fifty years of practice, research, and teaching in the field of addiction, Part One of this book will help the addicted person, significant others, and professionals who are likely to refer clients to alcohol and drug treatment sort through their options. It will aid you in choosing an approach that is both least intrusive and most likely to achieve a positive outcome.

We begin Part One by introducing you in chapter 2 to the range of traditional treatment services available and to the underlying principles upon which most of these treatment approaches are based. We then give an overview of the basic structure and configuration of activities within these various options. We also summarize today's major pharmacological approaches to substance dependency and discuss the role of 12-step groups in treatment and as aftercare strategies.

In chapters 3 and 4 we cover some of the major pros and cons of entering traditional treatment or participating in 12-step groups. Most persons are likely to have some familiarity with the advantages of enrolling in addiction treatment when it is thought to be necessary. They are less likely to be acquainted with the advantages of attending 12-step meetings. However, unbeknownst to most, there are also major disadvantages to participating in both of these forms of intervention. In these two chapters we will discuss what we believe to be the main advantages and disadvantages of entering formal treatment or participating in 12-step groups.

In chapter 5 we identify a range of emerging alternatives

to traditional addiction treatment and self-help. We introduce these alternatives in a way that will help inform you about nontraditional treatment possibilities and the increasing range of self-help options available. In this chapter we identify and discuss a number of new approaches, including Brief Interventions, Rational Recovery, Self-Management and Recovery Training, Women for Sobriety, Secular Organization for Sobriety, Moderation Management, and Drink Wise. We also show how access to these groups and other substance-dependency-related assistance can be found on the Internet at no cost.

In chapter 6 we discuss the various contexts within which addiction and resolution of drug problems occur. Substance dependency does not emerge in a vacuum isolated from the personal characteristics and environmental contexts of the user. Age, gender, values, available resources, severity of use, types of substances used, physical and mental health, as well as a range of other conditions are all factors that can influence how drugs affect people. In this chapter we discuss the relevance of such factors in planning an effective cessation strategy.

Chapter 7 is the last chapter in Part One. Here we identify strategies for selecting the least intrusive approach that will most likely render positive results with the least amount of adverse risks. In this chapter we encourage you to visit programs, treatment professionals, self-help meetings, and websites as part of your decision-making process. We explain methods for evaluating your fit with a particular program, including questions to ask the treatment staff. We also note the lack of alternative self-help groups in many communities and show how some of this limitation can be addressed by using the Internet.

Part Two of this book is directed to those who want to quit their destructive use of alcohol and other drugs but also want to avoid treatment and self-help groups altogether. Drawing on our research on natural recovery, we identify the major advantages of recovery without formal treatment or participation in self-help groups and introduce you to the types of people in our studies who were successful at it. In the bulk of Part Two we identify and discuss the principle strategies that were employed by these self-remitters at various stages of their efforts.

In chapter 8 we identify what we have found to be the major advantages of untreated recovery and introduce you to the characteristics of self-remitters, both those who have been identified by our own research as well as by the research of others who have studied natural recovery. We identify personal characteristics and social conditions that appear to foster a successful natural recovery.

In chapter 9 we discuss how you can begin a natural recovery effort. Here you will find the key issues that you should address as you contemplate this course of resolution. We identify the strategies that we have discovered, from our research and the research of others, to be essential in the early phase of this self-change process.

In chapter 10 we identify strategies that have been found to be particularly helpful in the latter phase of a successful natural recovery effort. For example, in this chapter we introduce you to the concept of conversion experience, the importance of engaging in meaningful work, methods for experiencing an improved sense of well-being without substance use, and other proven strategies.

Chapter 11 provides suggestions for successfully reintegrating yourself back into conventional society with a healthy perspective on your past life that had included alcohol and drugs. Here, both those who wish to adopt an abstinent lifestyle and those who opt for moderation will find helpful suggestions and information. In this chapter we also discuss the relevance of personal growth that goes far beyond merely arresting addiction, and we identify resources that we have found to be invaluable aids in assisting people in their efforts.

PART ONE

CONSUMERS' GUIDE TO ADDICTION TREATMENT

CHAPTER 2

Overview of Traditional Addiction Treatment

Addiction treatment in the United States has had a relatively short but interesting history. In the name of treating people for their drinking and drug habits, various approaches such as incarceration, whippings, and blood letting have been used. While such techniques may sound absurd today, these approaches were considered state-of-the-art in their time and can serve to remind us of the limitations associated with any accepted form of addiction treatment, even those used today.

While addiction treatment in the United States can be traced to the founding of this country, several twentieth-century events have had major influences on contemporary treatment, including the creation of two hospitals in 1935, one in Lexington, Kentucky, the other in Fort Worth,

Texas, to treat prison inmates for narcotic addiction; the founding of Alcoholics Anonymous (AA) that same year; the influence of Marty Mann, an early member of AA, and E. M. Jellinek in the 1950s to regard alcohol dependency as a disease that belongs in the sphere of medicine; the creation of the National Institute of Alcoholism and Alcohol Abuse (NIAAA) in 1970, which provides funds for alcohol dependency treatment; and the creation of the National Institute on Drug Abuse (NIDA) in 1975, which provides funding for drug abuse treatment. In fact, before the creation of NIAAA in 1970, treatment for substance dependency was primarily relegated to large, state-run mental health hospitals. The vestiges of these past events and procedures undergird most treatment programs across the country today. Due to developments in the past sixty years, treatment has primarily been seen as the province of medicine, with the view that addiction is a disease exerting a major influence over the way we treat addicted persons. The leading disease-based approach to addiction, Alcoholics Anonymous (AA), is currently a main staple of most treatment and aftercare programs.

In this chapter we identify traditional treatment services—approaches that are most widely available in the United States and that tend to approach addiction from similar ideological and theoretical frameworks. We also introduce you to the basic tenets of Alcoholics Anonymous and other 12-step groups and identify their influence on traditional addiction treatment.

Treatment

For the most part, treatment for alcohol and other drug dependencies has historically been in the form of inpatient care, where the client enters a program for a specified amount of time and undergoes various therapeutic experiences that are intended to address his or her substance dependency. When addiction treatment was primarily the responsibility of large state mental health hospitals, patient stay was approximately sixty days. More recently, as treatment became recognized as an insurable expense, the extent of coverage for treatment stay has been declining, primarily in an effort by insurance companies to contain costs. At one point, twenty-eight days of inpatient care was the norm as a reimbursable expense for substance abuse treatment services. Today, while there are some insurance plans that still pay for twenty-eight days of inpatient care, most coverage has been significantly reduced to cover fewer days, often a detoxification period of three to seven days coupled only with outpatient care. In terms of private inpatient care, most addiction services are now provided by managed care organizations (MCOs). While public programs can still offer more protracted inpatient treatment, many of these programs are guided by collaborative arrangements between the states, insurance companies, and MCOs. When this is not the case, limited funding and other financial restraints are forcing public programs to reduce the amount of care that they can offer substance-dependent clients.

More recently, however, cost containment measures by MCOs have led to a dramatic increase in outpatient services as well as a move toward such services in publicly funded programs. These outpatient services operate both from the traditional perspective and in more innovative, less traditional ways. We will briefly give an overview of traditional outpatient care in this chapter, but we will also discuss nontraditional outpatient services in chapter 5. Here we also survey detoxification, inpatient residential, therapeutic communities, and pharmacological approaches to treating substance dependency.

Detoxification

Detoxification (detox) is the beginning of treatment for some, though it may not be required in all cases. Detoxification is the process of gradually weaning a person off alcohol or other drugs. The procedure generally requires medical supervision and close monitoring of the patient since withdrawal from chronic use of certain substances can be dangerous and even life threatening. This danger is particularly significant for those habituated to large quantities of alcohol and other central nervous depressants such as barbiturates and tranquilizers. Various medications in conjunction with a regimen of vitamin and mineral therapy are often used to reduce the unpleasant effects of withdrawal symptoms. While some detoxification is done on an outpatient basis, most occurs in a hospital-type setting or in a closely monitored residential facility. Most detoxification programs have medical staff on site and twenty-four-hour medical assistance on call. Length of stay in a detoxification program can vary from three to four days to three to four weeks, but as indicated above, many stays are determined by policies set by insurance companies and MCOs. Many detoxification programs are attached to or are integral first step components of inpatient or residential programs.

Inpatient Residential

Inpatient residential programs require the person seeking help to become an inpatient or resident of their program, living at the facility for a specified period of time. Although the term "inpatient" generally denotes affiliation with a health-care agency, and "residential" suggests a less formal association with such institutions, the terms are often used interchangeably. The term "residential" is often also used to indicate that care is provided for extended periods. For example, therapeutic communities where persons often undergo treatment for a year or more are generally referred to as residential rather than inpatient programs. We use the term "inpatient residential" to refer to the range of these types of programs.

Like detoxification, inpatient residential facilities typically conduct an initial screening evaluation of the individual to determine if he or she is appropriate for the services offered by the particular program. Staff in these programs will also conduct more comprehensive assessments to determine the extent of the person's alcohol or drug problem, including how it has affected family, work, school, and other areas of the person's life. These assessments ordinarily require completion of questionnaires and face-to-face interviews with agency staff. Clients are generally diagnosed as exhibiting symptoms of either substance use, substance abuse, or substance dependency. More often than not, in order to qualify for inpatient residential care and for coverage by insurance or MCOs, the person has to meet the diagnostic criteria for the more severe condition of substance dependency. In some cases, admission to the program is dependent on the person meeting the criteria for other mental health conditions that are mandated by his or her insurance or MCO plan. Once admitted to an inpatient or residential program, the person can expect to participate in a variety of experiences with the intended outcome of eliminating a need for mind-altering substances.

In general, there is a set time for all residents to wake up and to take care of personal hygiene needs before eating breakfast. Residents are not allowed to sleep in, except under extraordinary circumstances. Some programs require residents to meet as a group before breakfast for light exercise, stretching, or other prebreakfast activities. Often, after breakfast, a morning meeting or other group activity will take place. In some programs this may include assigned chores or responsibilities such as cleaning, while in other programs there are therapeutic, educational, or informational meetings. Typically, between breakfast and lunch and lunch and dinner there are scheduled activities, primarily in a group format and for various purposes. These can include informational presentations, group therapy, other group activities, or individual assignments such as journaling and other kinds of writing or reading assignments. While residents may have some free time in the morning or afternoon hours, ordinarily free time occurs after dinner.

Most of the structured activities take place during daytime hours from Mondays to Fridays, when most of the professional staff are on site. At some point, residents will meet with their assigned counselors or therapists. In some treatment centers, counselors and professional staff are scheduled to have evening hours. During these sessions, and with input from the client, a treatment plan will typically be developed where individual goals and objectives are identified. Periodic assessment of the person's progress also occurs during these sessions. Most programs also provide an opportunity for physical examination by a health-care professional, which can take place on or off site; often, programs have arrangements with community health-care providers for this service.

Some facilities may offer similar structured activities on weekends and holidays, but often the programs operate on a modified schedule on those days. Some programs have only very few structured activities in place for clients during these times. Although this downtime offers relief from the rigors of a tight schedule for some, weekends and holidays can be particularly challenging for others due to boredom or loneliness. Some resourceful and creative programs turn weekends into an opportunity for activities that can be very enjoyable, such as field trips, various forms of entertainment, and family visits. Some treatment facilities are experimenting with creative program activities that provide unique rehabilitative opportunities for their clients.

Outpatient

Although persons have been seeking help for their substance misuse problems from psychotherapists since the inception of psychotherapy, the system of outpatient treatment services is a relatively new phenomenon in the United States. These services are generally thought to be more appropriate for those with less severe problems, those who are more socially stable or whose social situation does not require removal from home. Increasingly, however, outpatient treatment is also being offered to persons whose substance misuse problems might be characterized as severe. This situation has been created primarily by the cost-containment efforts of insurers and MCOs rather than through outpatient treatment-efficacy research.

Outpatient treatment programs for addiction can take place in private offices, hospital settings, and community agencies. Like inpatient residential treatment, outpatient treatment can have a range of intensity and duration. Some can take the form of a fifty-minute session with a counselor, social worker, psychologist, or other substance abuse treatment professionals once a week or biweekly. Other outpatient approaches, often referred to as intensive outpatient services, require the client to attend daily activities at the agency but not to remain overnight. In some intensive outpatient programs, these activities are only offered during evening hours. Outpatient services can range from a few hours or days of contact with the treatment provider to many months of such contact. Like inpatient residential services, clients are generally assigned a primary counselor and will be involved in various forms of educational or therapeutic group activities throughout the course of treatment. Outpatient clients are often encouraged to take advantage of other community resources, including attendance at self-help group meetings. While monitoring of substance use through periodic urine analysis occurs in inpatient residential programs, urine analysis is an integral component of most outpatient programs.

There are several distinct advantages of outpatient treatment. No matter who pays for these services, be it the individual client, the insurance company, or the MCO, or whether the services are provided by public agencies and paid for by the taxpayer, outpatient treatment is considerably less costly than inpatient residential treatment. As such, treatment can be extended for longer periods if necessary. Another advantage of outpatient services is that clients can continue to maintain family, work, and other responsibilities while receiving treatment. Clients also have the opportunity to apply what they have learned in treatment to real-life situations since they are not removed from their environments. On the other hand, clients have the opportunity to use alcohol and other drugs while undergoing treatment, which is a temptation that those in inpatient residential care may not face.

Therapeutic Communities

Therapeutic communities (TCs) are long-term residential treatment programs designed for those whose substance abuse problems are extremely severe and whose lives are intertwined with criminal activity of the street drug subculture. Typically, these programs are publicly funded and require a six- to eighteen-month commitment on the part of the client. If you include aftercare activities, involvement with these programs can take as long as three years; in some instances, a lifetime of association is expected. Although TCs are for volunteer clients, many serve primarily as an alternative to incarceration for those whose criminal offenses are related to their drug use. However, like many other approaches, they are inappropriate for those with significant health or mental health problems. TCs operate on a set of principles that can be perceived as incompatible with the ethical values associated with professions such as social work and psychological counseling. Residents are isolated from society and placed in a highly structured environment where they are resocialized into behaving in more responsible ways. This resocialization occurs through heavy-handed confrontation, group pressure, shared responsibilities, and a system of rewards and punishments.

A typical day for a resident in a therapeutic community is similar to that described for clients in residential care. However, much of the governance in TCs is done by the residents and by the hierarchy that is created among them as they progress through various levels of the program. Admission to the program can be an intense and sometimes intimidating experience, since some admission procedures require the applicant to seek the approval of the residents (also referred to as the family) through a group interview with them. The experience can be more of a function of who happens to be a resident at the time of the interview than on the ability of the applicant to demonstrate a need for and willingness to comply with treatment demands.

As in other approaches to addiction, persons have reported favorable as well as unfavorable experiences with TCs. Often those who successfully complete therapeutic community programs have very positive things to say about the TC experience. Conversely, many who drop out of these programs or otherwise fail at them are especially critical of them and their approach to addiction treatment. Recently, some of the confrontational and punishment tactics associated with the TCs have also received criticism from treatment professionals. These professionals assert that such tactics have not proved to be superior to other more conventional helping behaviors of counselors, social workers, therapists, and other mental health professionals. Whether one has positive or negative impressions of TCs, the therapeutic community approach is one of the most intrusive methods available to the substance-dependent person.

Pharmacological Approaches

Pharmacological approaches to treatment of substance abuse problems involve the administration of another drug to reduce or block the effects of the abused drug, to create an adverse unpleasant side effect when the abused drug is used, or to substitute for the abused drug. In some situations, these medication drugs are administered to ease the unpleasant physical symptoms of withdrawal or the psychological discomfort of discontinued substance use. The medication drug can be administered in a number of different kinds of ways and under various hospital, clinic, and community agency auspices. These medications may be administered as part of an inpatient or outpatient strategy treatment. It may be the primary course of treatment for an indefinite period of time, or used as part of a more comprehensive service and offered only on a short-term basis until the client is more stable. While most residential substance dependency treatment programs purport to be drug free, most of their detox strategies rely heavily on the administration of an assortment of medications to clients. Some programs include medications as strategic components of their aftercare approaches, and below we will survey several that are most widely used today.

Pharmacological approaches to substance misuse have primarily focused on dependence on alcohol and opiates. More recently, medications have been introduced to combat dependence on cocaine and other powerful stimulants. Strategies most widely used today include primarily the administration of antabuse (disulfiram), methadone, naltrexone, and buprenorphine.

The most popular pharmacological approach to alcohol dependence is the administration of antabuse. It is taken daily, and when used in combination with alcohol the results can be extremely unpleasant. Effects include facial flushing, nausea, vomiting, difficulty in breathing, and other aversive symptoms. Antabuse is considered a deterrent against drinking alcohol and a temporary aid for difficult times when the urge to drink is strong. Naltrexone, principally used in treating opiate dependence, has recently shown some promise in treating alcohol dependence. While not as well known as antabuse treatment, naltrexone therapy is becoming increasingly available at various treatment programs across the United States. Naltrexone diminishes the effects of alcohol on the user, thereby making alcohol use less desirable. Proponents of naltrexone therapy claim that it also reduces cravings for alcohol use. Both of these drugs may be administered as a primary intervention or as an adjunct to more comprehensive treatment.

Methadone is a synthetic opiate that is used in the treatment of opiate addiction, primarily heroin dependence. It is used both to detoxify persons from their dependence on other opiates and to maintain them on an adequate level of an opiate for indefinite periods of time to prevent withdrawal symptoms and promote life stability. In the case of detoxification, decreasing doses of methadone are administered until the person is weaned off the drug altogether. Methadone maintenance provides opiate-dependent persons with a steady daily dose for a long time, in some cases for life. Methadone maintenance programs also provide people the opportunity to stabilize their lives and assume regular responsibilities since they no longer need to raise large sums of money (often through criminal activity) to support their heroin habits. Once they are stabilized on an appropriate dose of methadone, they will benefit from its effects generally for twenty-four to thirty-six hours, requiring only one dose a day. A longer-acting form of methadone, known as LAMM (l-alpha-acetyl-methadol), produces effects that last more than seventy-two hours, thus requiring doses to be given only every two or three days. Since methadone is taken orally, its use removes many of the dangers associated with injection of opiates. Methadone maintenance programs range from those that primarily dispense the drug with very little counseling or other supportive services, to those that offer a wide range of individual, group, family, vocational, and educational services.

As with most approaches to substance dependency, methadone maintenance programs are not without their critics. Some writers on the subject see the substitution of one opiate for another as wrong, and others think that methadone is a much more addictive drug with much greater associated withdrawal symptoms and should not be substituted for less potent opiates with less severe related withdrawal symptoms. Still others question whether methadone maintenance really benefits the opiate-dependent person or if in reality actually responds to the interests of the larger society at the expense of extreme dependency on methadone by opiate-dependent persons.

Naltrexone therapy is becoming increasingly available at clinics and in treatment programs and is being seen as an alternative to methadone maintenance. As in the case of the reduced effects of alcohol upon ingestion, naltrexone blocks the effects of opiates. It is a relatively long-acting medication, with one dose blocking the effects of heroin from twenty-four to seventy-two hours, depending on the quantity of the heroin. Naltrexone can be administered once every two days.

Buprenorphine therapy is probably best characterized as an emerging rather than an established approach. Though it is still not widely available, it is now being administered in some of the traditional treatment settings discussed in this chapter. Administration of buprenorphine is an approach that seems to hold promise for addressing opiate as well as cocaine dependence. Its action is similar to that of naltrexone in that it blocks the effects of the opiate on the user. For those who stop cocaine use, buprenorphine will also reduce the cravings associated with cocaine withdrawal. Both naltrexone and buprenorphine are dispensed as a primary course of treatment as well as an adjunct to other types of treatment.

12-Step Groups

Most current treatment programs utilize some degree of 12-step group involvement in their protocols, and in some such involvement is an integral component of treatment. Attendance at 12-step meetings is encouraged, and sometimes required, as part of the treatment and/or aftercare. Some programs actually base much of their program planning around 12-step activities that are to be carried out throughout the day. The Hazelden Program, also known as the Minnesota

Model, draws heavily on 12-step doctrine and language. Many treatment programs emulate this treatment model across the United States, including the well-known Betty Ford Clinic in California.

Alcoholics Anonymous (AA), founded in 1935, is the template for all 12-step programs. Some of the most recent offshoots of AA include Narcotics Anonymous, Cocaine Anonymous, and Over-eaters Anonymous, to name a few. These groups slightly modify the language set forth in the 12-steps of AA to meet their unique needs, but the content and its disease-based views are virtually all the same. AA is a loose network of self-help support groups available for persons who want to stop their destructive consumption of alcohol. The support offered is primarily in the form of meetings where persons learn the 12-steps of AA and how to apply them in their attempts to stop alcohol addiction. Meetings are widely available across the nation and in other countries around the globe. In major urban centers and larger cities one can find an AA meeting almost at any hour of the day or night.

The main principles of AA and other information about the organization can be found on its website: www.alcoholics-anonymous.org. These principles, what members refer to as the 12-steps, are as follows:

1. We admitted that we were powerless over alcohol—that our lives had become unmanageable.
2. Came to believe that a Power greater than ourselves could restore us to sanity.

3. Made a decision to turn our will and our lives over to the care of God as we understood Him.

4. Made a searching and fearless moral inventory of ourselves.

5. Admitted to God, to ourselves, and to another human being the exact nature of our wrongs.

6. Were entirely ready to have God remove all these defects of character.

7. Humbly asked Him to remove our shortcomings.

8. Made a list of all persons we had harmed, and became willing to make amends to them all.

9. Made direct amends to such people wherever possible, except when to do so would injure them or others.

10. Continued to take a personal inventory and when we were wrong promptly admitted it.

11. Sought through prayer and meditation to improve our conscious contact with God as we understood Him, praying only for His will for us and the power to carry that out.

12. Having had a spiritual awakening as the result of these steps, we tried to carry the message to alcoholics, and to practice these principles in all our affairs.

The phrase "as we understood Him" in steps 3 and 11 were not in the original 12-steps but were added later to reflect tolerance of divergent views of the concept of God. They are highlighted in original printed materials in italics.

While the founders of AA probably never intended for its 12-steps to serve as formal treatment, particularly treatment for profit delivered by certified counselors, social workers, psychologists, and other trained professionals, they do serve as the philosophical, and often structural, frameworks for many programs in the United States. The influence of the tenets of AA on traditional treatment can vary enormously. Some programs might simply suggest to their clients that they consider attending 12-step meetings upon completion of treatment, while other programs provide guidance and leadership in such activities as "step work," "studying the big book," and other planned 12-step-related activities.

Conclusion

What we have presented in this chapter should in no way be seen as an exhaustive review of traditional treatment approaches to addiction. There are simply too many substance-abuse treatment programs and professionals who practice in the field to capture the entire scope of treatment today. Furthermore, many of the traditional approaches are evolving into different forms of treatment. For example, although the disease theory of addiction continues to dominate most treatment programs, many are now using cognitive and social learning approaches that do not so readily accept the dogma associated with the traditional disease views of addiction. Others are drawing on a combination of biological, psychological, and social theories to guide their practice with substance-dependent clients. Still others, many of which we review later in this book, are beginning to experiment with alternative treatment strategies. A number of traditional programs are also beginning to experiment with medications not discussed above, in addition to a range of vitamin, mineral, and nutritional therapies. However, though it is not possible to cover all that goes on in traditional treatment, we have presented here an overview of the bulk of the treatment world in America. In the next two chapters, we take an even closer look at traditional treatment and 12-step programs and consider the various pros ands cons of these approaches. In chapter 7 we will go into detail about ways to locate and enter these various treatment options.

CHAPTER 3

Pros and Cons of Entering Traditional Treatment

Today, it would be impossible to estimate with any degree of accuracy how many persons in the United States have undergone some form of formal inpatient or outpatient treatment to remedy substance abuse problems. What we can say is that the number is in the many millions. Although participation has been high, estimates about success vary widely. Most addiction and treatment researchers would agree that although many people have been helped, the unfortunate reality is that the majority return to problematic substance use after treatment. Equally disturbing, and perhaps somewhat surprising, is the fact that many people who have undergone treatment have had very negative experiences. In this chapter, we identify the various pros and cons of enrolling in traditional addiction treatment. We present opposing viewpoints to assist you when considering what treatment to choose for yourself or someone else.

Pros of Treatment

Seeing Others in Treatment

Unless a person receives only individual counseling or psychotherapy for substance dependency, one of the first things the person realizes when entering treatment is that he or she is not alone with this problem. There are many others who are experiencing similar problems and are seeking formal help to resolve their addictions. This firsthand personal experience can be comforting to those who feel alone in their situations and have hesitated in taking action to resolve their problems. Excessive and destructive use of alcohol and other drugs can carry with it feelings of isolation and guilt around secrecy that are often reduced when the substance-dependent person actually enters a situation where there are others who have traveled the same path and are now taking action. It can be very motivating to see others who share your struggle and to recognize that you are not alone.

Access to Experts

Many who enter treatment often are oblivious to the actual pharmacological actions of various drugs, how to best approach eliminating use of these substances, how to maintain gains that are made, and how to enjoy life without alcohol or other drugs. Through counseling, psychotherapy, group work, and other structured activities, individuals in these programs are exposed to information that might not otherwise be available to them. As part of their requirements for retaining their practice credentials, many addiction professionals attend workshops and conferences where they are often exposed to promising new treatment techniques that can be applied in their own practice. Some of these counselors are also available to offer valuable personal support during moments of ambivalence or other difficult times. Counselors who have experienced substance-abuse-related difficulties themselves may serve as role models for getting over these problems and living a productive life. Drawing on their education, ongoing training, and, in many cases, their own successes at overcoming alcohol and other drug addictions, skilled treatment providers can assist those who seek help for their substance dependency problems.

Sometimes the kind of assistance discussed above can actually come from others enrolled in the treatment program. This can be especially true in residential programs where participants spend a great deal of time around one another through structured as well as unstructured activities. Other program participants provide newer clients with valuable information and subtle insights into the process of quitting and how best to take advantage of what the program has to offer. As with the counselors, they too can provide helpful support to other clients during difficult periods and model behaviors that can aid the recovery process.

Help with Other Aspects of Life

Many treatment programs also offer an array of services that support treatment for alcohol and drug problems but also provide important information and promote skills that could improve the quality of other areas of the drug user's life. Some programs offer comprehensive physical and mental health examinations that can uncover important information about an individual's health and mental status that might have gone undetected under ordinary circumstances. Assertiveness training, relaxation techniques, and other life-enhancing skills are often introduced to individuals in some of these programs. Information about nutrition and wellness is offered at programs that emphasize these aspects of quitting. Some of the more resourceful programs introduce their clients to various sport, leisure, educational, and recreational activities that can be of enormous benefit to any person. Through casework methods, good programs will connect addicted people to other types of services besides those offered by their agency—services that can be helpful in addressing broader problem areas of a person's life. Assessments for and referrals to services provided by other community agencies, such as those that provide educational and vocational services, represent the kinds of referral relationships that substance abuse treatment agencies can have.

Work with Families

Families can play an integral role in the creation, maintenance, and resolution of a substance abuse problem for the substance-dependent family member. Comprehensive programs will offer some type of assistance to these families, and they can range from the educational to the therapeutic. Such services might include exposing the client to educational materials about the harm of excessive alcohol and drug use, or they could take the form of family work directed toward helping the family make the necessary adjustments that facilitate, rather than impede, the recovery process. These services can also help families cope with the uncertainty of change and with confusion about their own roles in the recovery process. Some programs offer therapy to family members in an effort to delve into the complex dynamics that relate to the substance dependency problem within the family. The results of this kind of family work can leave lasting impressions on the way family members relate to one another in a variety of ways, not only in matters that pertain to substance misuse, but also to broader issues such as communication, power dynamics, and household responsibilities.

Interruption of Access and Routines

Those who enter treatment, particularly inpatient residential programs, become severely restricted in their access to alcohol and other drugs, and daily routines that support drug use are disrupted. These changes are important. Easy access to drugs can play a major role in preventing people from quitting. Even when they have a sincere desire to stop drinking alcohol or taking other drugs, the wide availability of alcohol or easy access to other drugs makes interruption of these behaviors particularly difficult. Furthermore, some drug users live in an environment where heavy alcohol or illicit drug use is an integral part of day-to-day life. These situations present significant barriers to those who want to end their addiction—both in terms of motivation as well as opportunities to do so. Being in treatment, if only for a brief period, may be a person's first opportunity to break the cycle of addiction.

Outpatient programs provide a different approach to breaking the cycle. Like many residential programs, outpatient treatment can introduce clients to skills that enable them to avoid drug-taking situations or techniques that increase the probability that they will be able to refuse alcohol and other drugs that may be offered to them. While this strategy might not appear to be as effective as an inpatient residential approach, advocates of outpatient programs propose that immediate opportunities to practice skills learned in treatment in the client's natural environment might be an even better strategy than isolation from drugs and the cues that encourage their use. Generally, however, both inpatient residential and outpatient substance abuse treatment programs monitor their clients' substance misuse through urine analysis, Breathalyzer tests, and other techniques. In outpatient programs, these procedures are relied upon more heavily to measure client progress or lack of progress than in programs where clients live at the facility. Many residential facilities also ask their clients to participate in their outpatient aftercare programs once they have completed inpatient treatment.

Health

When people are involved in a lifestyle of heavy consumption of alcohol and drugs, their health is often severely compromised. A frequently overlooked benefit of inpatient residential programs is that treatment provides an opportunity to begin to rebuild health. While a focus on health varies from program to program, simply being away from the alcohol and drug scene in a treatment program can in itself result in improved health for program participants. In addition to receiving physical and mental health examinations offered in many programs, residents will also begin to improve their eating habits.

Program scheduling that roughly delineates sleep and waking hours also contributes to the improved health of residential clients. Many heavy drug users, particularly those who use stimulants such as cocaine and methamphetamines, develop sleep patterns that have put inordinate stress on the body. Returning to a normal pattern of sleep does much to restore the body's health and promote a sense of well-being. As already mentioned, the recreational activities offered by some programs also hold promise for promoting good health.

Cons of Treatment

Before starting this discussion, we feel it is important to state that, although we have discussed in chapter 2 what we mean by the term "traditional treatment," we are aware that treatment programs across the United States can vary enormously. And, although most of these programs are driven by the disease theory of drug dependency, many draw on a range of other theories to create program activities and meet program goals of eliminating addiction in their clients. Treatment professionals who practice in these settings also draw on a wide range of other theories when working with persons experiencing drug problems. Therefore, the weaknesses of traditional treatment that we discuss below are best seen as observations about the general state of conventional addiction treatment in America rather than blanket statements that apply to all facilities or to a specific alcohol and drug treatment program. Some treatment programs are currently advancing promising innovative treatment strategies.

One Size Fits All

While approaches may vary across programs, one of the principle criticisms of addiction treatment is that most of the programs treat people with alcohol and drug problems in a similar, if not the same, way. Even programs that purport to design their treatment intervention to meet the specific needs of the individual experiencing problems tend to remain faithful to a standardized course of treatment activities. Although professionals, such as psychologists and licensed clinical social workers, may have undergone training that underscores the critical role that gender, class, and other socio-demographic characteristics play in creating and sustaining dysfunctional behavior, much of this diversity perspective gets ignored within actual treatment. For some of these professionals, the assumption that addiction is a disease shared by all addicted persons supersedes any differences they might have.

This standardized method has also resulted in a universal goal for nearly all addicted persons in these programs. Any goal short of abstinence is generally not seen as a legitimate expected outcome by those who staff the programs. The abstinence imperative includes abstinence from all mind-altering substances (except caffeine and nicotine) for the addicted person. While this might be an appropriate expectation for some, for others such a rigid and perhaps unrealistic goal could be inappropriate. Even when treatment providers recognize that reduction is a more appropriate objective than abstinence, other forces, such as the criminal justice system and other community-based services connected with treatment, restrict its implementation.

The major barrier to more individualized treatment relates to an overreliance on the disease view of addiction by most treatment programs. This orientation dictates a circumscribed course of treatment that limits options and inhibits flexibility around specific strategies that substance-dependent persons need to employ to get better. Even programs designed for adolescents tend to approach treatment of alcohol and drug problems from a disease perspective. Such approaches severely restrict innovation and versatility to the point that some youth programs look like adult programs and, as a result, may not be realistic for young people approaching adulthood.

Another impediment to individualized approaches is that much of the activity in treatment programs is carried out in group format, which means that all of the program participants get exposed to the same educational or therapeutic content during the group sessions. While this might be an efficient strategy, it nonetheless creates barriers for more person-specific strategies.

Because most paraprofessionals who staff these programs were at some point themselves participants in these standardized formats during their own treatment experiences, they have tended to institutionalize this one-size-fits-all approach within and across programs. If these counselors have personally benefited from such a course of treatment, it is easy to see how difficult it would be to alter the process. However, while seeing the results of success in treatment can be of value to those currently enrolled in it, a particular counselor's success story can actually misrepresent the rate of success for that treatment. The simple fact is that far many more persons fail at substance abuse treatment than succeed.

Being Labeled an Alcoholic or Drug Addict for Life

Whether one enters a public or private addiction treatment program, an assessment and/or diagnosis of substance dependency must be made. In other words, in order to receive this service, you must demonstrate that you actually qualify for it. On its face this seems reasonable. However, because the disease view of substance dependency is so pervasive in the treatment community and has been conveyed to the general public by the popular media, diagnosis of drug dependency can carry with it profound and lifelong implications.

The disease theory of addiction postulates that if you are addicted, you have inherited or, through your substance misuse, have contracted the disease of addiction. This view also assumes that the disease of addiction that you have is progressive, that it gets worse over time. It also postulates that there is no real cure for your disease, even if you stop using alcohol and other drugs. It suggests that during abstinence your disease is merely in a dormant state of remission and will return to its active state if you take a drink or use a mind-altering drug. In other words, the disease view maintains that you are an alcoholic and/or a drug addict and will be one for the rest of your life. The problem with taking on these life-long labels and pessimistic assumptions is that they are by-products of this theory of addiction, a theory that has not been substantiated by scientific research and one that is actually receiving more and more criticism from researchers who study addiction and the recovery process. For the more severely addicted person who has been habituated to alcohol or other drugs for many years, who has been in and out of various treatment programs, and whose health has been severely compromised by chronic use, such labels and beliefs may, in some cases, be beneficial, at least for a period of time. But, for the majority of substance abusers whose level of use is not that extensive and whose deterioration is not that profound, disease-based beliefs and the related identity of being a life-long alcoholic or drug addict is often counterproductive.

Although the influence of the disease theory of addiction exercises considerable sway over current alcohol and drug treatment programs, the degree to which programs subscribe to this view vary. Those that draw heavily on the Minnesota Model or the philosophy of 12-step groups are likely to strictly adhere to the tenets of the disease theory. Other programs that rely more on theories that emanate from the social sciences, such as psychology and sociology, are less likely to be overly influenced by the disease theory. It is important to note, however, that entering treatment for substance dependency can result in being labeled an alcoholic or drug addict, a designation that can follow you the rest of your life.

Privacy and Your Future

Entering a substance dependency treatment program results in documentation of your addiction and a formal record of your treatment for this condition. A number of unanticipated consequences may result. Although medical records are considered confidential, if your treatment is paid for by an insurance company, others beyond the treatment personnel have access to documentation that you have undergone treatment for alcoholism or drug addiction. A little-known fact is that most insurance companies, through the Medical Information Bureau, have access to a large database of every claim filed for medical and mental health care. Claims filed

43

for substance abuse treatment exist in that database and are accessed by carriers to determine premium rates for its subscribers. Because of the view promoted by treatment providers and 12-step groups that substance dependency is a lifelong disease, even if one has had only a short bout with cocaine, for example, one may pay higher premiums for life.

Applications for insurance or increased insurance—even increased mortgage insurance—include questions about one's substance abuse treatment history, as do applications for all sorts of other services and opportunities, as well. Job applications, admissions to various educational programs, licensure and certification applications, and a host of other application processes include questions about one's substance abuse treatment history. While in rare cases such information may be prudent (e.g., application for a pilot's position with a commercial airline), we see little reason why one episode of treatment should influence these various applications for a lifetime. Thus, those who have undergone formal treatment for an alcohol or drug problem have little protection of privacy against such unreasonable requests.

Effectiveness of Treatment

Perhaps one of the most disappointing realities about treatment for alcohol and other drug dependencies in America is the very high likelihood that treatment will not solve one's substance abuse problem. While research findings on the effectiveness of treatment vary, there is considerable scientific evidence that most persons will resolve their substance dependency problem without undergoing treatment. There are several studies that even suggest that one's chances of overcoming substance dependence with treatment is no better than it is for those who do not undergo treatment at all.

One should note, however, that while success may not be achieved during one's treatment experience, people often receive information or learn skills in treatment that will eventually aid them in a recovery effort. Some may benefit from treatment by being removed from the dangers of increased use or continued exposure the using world. If quitting is not achieved, the motivation to quit may not have been sufficiently high or conditions were not exactly right the first time around. Nonetheless, it is critically important that consumers of treatment services know that entering conventional treatment is very likely to result in a return to use and dependency rather than abstinence.

Treatment Driven by Insurance and Managed Care

Currently, insurance companies and MCOs are having an enormous impact on the delivery of addiction treatment in the United States. Some of the many disadvantages of current treatments are directly related to this new financing arrangement. Regardless of the effectiveness or ineffectiveness of an approach, the specific course of addiction treatment that one receives today is driven more by guidelines set by insurance companies and MCOs than by individual need. These guidelines tend to be overly restrictive since they are influenced more by cost-containment objectives than by the quality of care that clients receive. Although at one time this kind of influence over treatment only affected private programs, currently such guidelines exercise considerable influence over the kinds of services available in many public programs. Some states provide health care, including treatment, to its public-sector clients or those not covered by insurance or MCOs through arrangements with insurance companies.

Unless the claimant is willing to pay for his or her own treatment services, these guidelines essentially inform decisions about what options are and are not available to him or her. Such policies determine whether or not the person is allowed to enter detoxification, inpatient residential, or outpatient treatment. If detoxification or inpatient residential is allowed, the guidelines dictate how long the person can be in such treatment. If only outpatient services are paid for, a specified number of sessions are generally allowed. And, since profit is the driving force behind these decisions, it is easy to see how the intensity, duration, and overall quality of treatment services are being severely compromised by the involvement of insurance companies and MCOs. If you or someone close to you plans to cover the expenses of treatment through these health benefits, it is essential that you understand these drawbacks.

Conclusion

In presenting the pros and cons of conventional treatment for alcohol and drug problems, we have deliberately been more general than specific in our observations since the universe of treatment programs is vast indeed. And, while traditional programs generally operate from the same philosophical framework of addiction, they vary in their structure and the way they deliver treatment services. We have presented the pros and cons only of treatments that we think are the most important for you to be aware of as you contemplate a decision about what to do for yourself or for someone you care about. We have attempted to present these competing viewpoints in a balanced way so that your decision about treatment is one that is most beneficial to you.

CHAPTER 4

Pros and Cons of Participating in 12-Step Groups

The role that 12-step groups play in attempting to help people overcome addiction to alcohol and other drugs is enormous. Such programs are regarded by many as a major component of the formal and informal infrastructure of treatment. While many treatment programs encourage or require their clients to attend 12-step meetings, many substance-dependent persons attend such meetings on their own without formal contact with treatment facilities. Yet, 12-step programs are not without their critics. Many of their most ardent detractors feel that these programs actually do more harm than good. Conversely, there are many fervent supporters of 12-step programs who feel that this method of recovery is the only path out of addiction. Here we will inform you of the more widely known pros and cons of participating in these groups.

Pros of Participating in 12-Step Groups

Wide Availability of 12-Step Groups

Twelve-step groups are widely available across the United States. Although small donations are usually collected at the conclusion of meetings, no fee is charged to attend meetings. In large metropolitan areas you can find a 12-step meeting almost at any hour of the day or night, seven days a week. The variety of groups in some urban areas is very large. These meetings include Alcoholics Anonymous, Narcotics Anonymous, Cocaine Anonymous, and a range of other 12-step group meetings. In some cities you may be able to find meetings that are more specific to your personal characteristics and lifestyle. If you search, you may find non-smokers meetings, all-women's meetings, meetings that cater to professionals, and so on. Although in rural areas the variety of groups will not be as large, you can generally find at least an AA meeting within a reasonable driving distance. When you are away from home, if you feel you want or need to attend a meeting, usually all you need to do is look in the phone book. There are even 12-step meetings available in some foreign countries.

Access to Social Support

Although most 12-step groups adhere to the disease explanation of addiction, most of the help that is actually provided is through social support. This support comes in the form of face-to-face group meetings and other activities outside of these meetings. Meetings offer an opportunity for one to openly discuss his or her alcohol and other drug problems with others who share similar difficulties. By helping each other apply the 12-steps to their individual lives, participants attempt to help each other resolve their substance dependency problems. By providing information about how they have personally managed to stay sober or clean, members teach and encourage each other to stay the course. Those who continue to participate in these groups generally welcome newcomers. The principle criterion for acceptance is a desire to stop drinking and/or using other mind-altering drugs. Unless there is some question about the appropriateness of someone new joining these groups, most participants are usually friendly toward newcomers.

A range of ongoing informal activities also brings participants together. These include social get-togethers such as weekend picnics, non-drinking or non-drug-using dances, parties, and other recreational activities. Some members become involved in the formal organizational structure of Alcoholics Anonymous or Narcotics Anonymous and find these activities socially rewarding.

Access to a Mentor

Sponsorship offers an opportunity for social as well as individual support through mentoring relationships. Sponsors serve as mentors to those with less 12-step experience and are available for guidance and support throughout the course of their participation in these groups. In many instances, the mentoring relationship between the sponsor and the member provides more social support and guidance for remedying the substance dependency problem than attendance at meetings. In some cases, these mentoring relationships go far beyond one's continued participation in 12-step meetings. Sponsors can provide a range of assistance, from how to apply the 12-steps to one's situation, to sharing their own strategies for recovery, to simply listening to the struggle being experienced by the newer member. The mentoring that comes with the sponsor relationship is a process that plays an integral role in the 12-step participant's success or lack of success.

Conversely, the act of serving as a sponsor to a newer member can bring with it a great sense of satisfaction. Serving as a counselor, a role model, a confidant, and providing other valuable services to someone in need of support can be extremely gratifying. The intrinsic benefits derived from helping others, and of giving of oneself, can be a potent reward and a key motivating factor for the sponsor to continue the course, too.

Access to Network of Nonusing Persons

Our research and the research of others have demonstrated that those persons who are successful at overcoming addiction often sever their relationships or restrict their contacts with those who continue to use. Of course, the down side of this strategy is that as social beings we will miss these relationships and will experience a noticeable void in our lives if we do not replace them with others. Often, people develop or rekindle friendships with family, old friends, work acquaintances, and other persons who do not use or use only socially to meet this basic human need. In some instances this transition is an easy one to make, though in others garnering these relationships is not as easy as it might appear. Becoming a member of a 12-step group automatically puts you in contact with a preexisting network of others who no longer use alcohol and other drugs. The seeds of many longtime acquaintances and friendships are born at some 12-step meetings. These relationships can go a long way in filling the void left by breaking away from substance-using relationships and networks. Such relationships exercise considerable influence over one's behavior and can also serve as a strong disincentive when faced with the urge to use again.

Compatibility with Religious Beliefs

Many persons in America are raised in families where religion is a central part of family life. Very often, persons veer away from their religious roots as they become more and more entangled in the world of alcohol and other drugs. Participation in 12-step programs offers one the opportunity to reconnect or reaffirm his or her faith through application of the 12-steps. For many, during this time of deep despair and anguish, a reconnection with one's fundamental faith can be extremely fulfilling, providing a sense of relief and solace that is liberating.

Help with Other Aspects of Life

Some who participate in AA, NA, and other 12-step groups state that the principles to which they were exposed through their participation in these groups actually helped them in other areas of their lives, beyond those related to substance use. The 12-steps, the principles inherent in them, the various discussions at meetings, and other experiences related to their participation in these groups can be drawn upon to improve other aspects of one's life. Even the various slogans that have emerged from the 12-step culture are credited with improving the quality of overall life for some. Slogans like "One day at a time," "Let go and let God," and "Easy does it," for example, have been reported as being useful in tempering the impact of other unpleasant circumstances in which participants may find themselves.

These are just a few of the pros that some see as important considerations for those contemplating joining 12-step groups. If you spoke with their members, you would no doubt hear other positive reasons for joining them.

Cons of Participating in 12-Step Groups

While 12-step groups offer a different kind of experience than formal treatment, treatment programs have adopted many of the principles espoused by 12-step groups. And, as you will see, many of the criticisms that persons have leveled at specific treatments have also been expressed about participation in 12-step groups. You may also notice that many of the advantages that some see in joining these groups are what others see as disadvantages. Opinions can vary sharply about the value of participating in 12-step groups.

The Principle of Powerlessness

Step 1 of AA reads, "We admitted that we were powerless over alcohol—that our live had become unmanageable." Many people have difficulty accepting this principle. Throughout our lives we are encouraged to believe that we are responsible for our own behavior, situations in which we find ourselves, and our overall life destinies. We are inculcated with the belief that if we study hard, postpone gratification, make responsible decisions, and so on, we can be successful at whatever it is that we want from life. The idea of powerlessness and lack of choice in contemporary America is simply counterintuitive for many people. Most believe that they are responsible for and in control of their own destinies. The notion of a future beyond one's control is too unsettling for most.

Others suggest that the powerlessness principle is simply an excuse for acting irresponsibly and selfishly, of not exercising restraint in the face of potential danger or harm to others. Some critics assert that those who allow themselves to become substance dependent are simply greedy, that they want to stay "high" all of the time; so much so, that eventually their bodies adjust to alcohol or other drugs and become dependent on these substances for normal functioning. Some critics contend that in reality people become substance dependent because of poor decision making, not powerlessness.

Religious Nature of 12-Step Groups

It is hard to know whether the concept of powerlessness or the religious underpinning of 12-step groups is the most disturbing for those who have difficulty with these groups. What we can say with some degree of confidence is that these two tenets are generally the first to be criticized by those who have negative views of 12-step groups. Most AA meetings begin with a recitation of the Serenity Prayer and conclude with the Lord's Prayer, and most of the 12-steps include a religious reference. Terms such as higher power, prayer, spiritual awakening, and God that are part of the language of the 12-steps can present huge barriers for some. For many, the idea that overcoming addiction is somehow tied to religious beliefs is unpalatable, if not objectionable. Many who do not believe in a supreme entity or hold atheist views find the 12-step approach offensive or unhelpful. Even those who hold religious beliefs often see the intermingling of religious tenets with overcoming substance dependence as a questionable enterprise.

Supporters of the 12-step approach assert that 12-step meetings are more spiritual than religious, and that one need not believe in God to fully benefit from this approach. Conversely, and perhaps expectedly, critics say that this might be true in some cases, but, overall, such claims are false and the term "spiritual" is an attempt to disguise the fact that the concept of a Judeo-Christian God is central in the practice of 12-step principles.

Addiction as a Disease

Many people find it objectionable that AA and other 12-step groups operate from the premise that addiction is a disease. (In fact, treatment as we know it today borrowed this perspective from AA rather than the other way around.) The proposition that substance dependency is a chronic and progressive disease and that it gets worse over time can be a hard pill to swallow. While many with long histories of substance dependency and numerous unsuccessful efforts to stop or cut back might find some psychological comfort in the position that addiction is a disease, innumerable others who have had similar problems and resolved them find this position troubling. The illness perspective calls one's attention to pessimistic images of deficit rather than competence, of pathology rather than wellness, and of weakness rather than strength. It is easy to see why persons who are optimistic and have a strong sense of self-efficacy find the disease view of substance dependency incompatible with their own views of how things work in the world. Twelve-step groups do not waver on their position about the cause of substance dependency; for them, this condition is a disease—straight and simple.

In some cases, the belief in addiction as a disease may become self-fulfilling, leading people to believe they have no ability to control their consumption practices. Indeed, in such cases, the addiction-as-a-disease view can have devastating results as it may contribute to continued excessive use since it accepts the myth of powerlessness.

Being Labeled an Alcoholic or Drug Addict for Life

The disease explanation of substance dependency is the driving force behind the equally disturbing belief promoted by 12-step groups that "once an addict, always an addict." Although treatment programs are also partially responsible for promulgation of this belief—a belief not supported by scientific research—12-step groups probably do more to attach permanent labels to drug-dependent persons than any other possible source. In fact, when persons introduce themselves or speak at AA meetings it is customary for them to state their first name and identify themselves as alcoholics. The typical introduction is, for example, "Hello. My name is John and I'm an alcoholic." In other meetings the practice is the same but the label is different. For example, in NA meetings, instead of John referring to himself as an alcoholic, he would refer to himself as an addict. Many persons reject being thought of as an alcoholic or a drug addict for the remainder of their lives. Some find that even associating with persons who see themselves as forever addicted is potentially harmful to their own recovery.

Abstinence as the Only Goal

While many have begun to challenge the goal of abstinence, 12-step groups continue to view it as the only worthy success marker. In fact, many members object to the taking of any kind of drug, including those to treat mental-health-related conditions.

The more ardent critics of 12-step groups assert that the strict adherence to abstinence is a hollow and unrealistic position to hold, and that many who attend 12-step meetings still continue to have serious addictions to nicotine and caffeine. Some go on to point to research findings that conclude that deaths directly related to nicotine dependence far exceed those related to addiction to alcohol and all other drugs combined, and that to condone this type of destructive drug taking is unconscionable.

Addiction to the Group

An addiction to the group might seem minor when contrasted to other addictions. Still, some critics of 12-step groups and even some more supportive of them have observed what they see as "addiction to the group"—an overreliance on participation in 12-step groups that compromises one's other important responsibilities. These people suggest that the participant has simply supplanted his or her dependency on alcohol and/or other drugs with inordinate levels of participation in 12-step meetings.

Conclusion

Any discussion about what can be done when faced with an addiction will necessarily include a discussion of 12-step groups such as AA and NA. The prominent place that these groups occupy within the realm of substance dependency interventions puts them at the center of any consideration about a possible course of action. Although there are other self-help groups that do not subscribe to the 12-step philosophy or otherwise differ from them (see chapter 5), no self-help group is as established or has had the impact on the world of alcohol and drug dependency as Alcoholics Anonymous.

We hope that what you have read in this chapter will assist you as you try to sort out an appropriate course of action for yourself or someone you care about. The pros and cons of 12-step programs that we discuss are not simply our opinions about these groups; they also reflect the opinions of many who have actually participated in the programs. These views have also been reported in the professional literature and can be found in various substance dependency treatment books.

CHAPTER 5

New and Emerging Approaches to Quitting

In the previous three chapters, our discussions focused on traditional addiction treatment programs and 12-step groups. Although these approaches continue to dominate the landscape of addiction treatment, and in most communities are the only readily available forms of help, there is a growing array of new and innovative approaches. While most treatment programs continue to subscribe exclusively to the disease explanation of addiction, some are slowly recognizing the value of these fresh approaches and are including some aspects of them as part of their treatment strategies or as referral sources for their clients. In this chapter we look at some of these promising new approaches.

An innovation taking place in some parts of the United States that is widely accessible in many communities is the formation of new groups dedicated to exploring alternative approaches to resolving addiction. Some of these groups depart sharply from the disease views associated with treatment and 12-step groups. In this chapter, we will identify these groups and tell you how to access them.

Among formal treatment options, far less innovation seems to be occurring in inpatient residential treatment settings than in outpatient programs. This contrast is especially apparent in private practice outpatient settings where counseling or psychotherapy is provided by professionals such as psychologists, licensed clinical social workers, and other highly trained clinicians. Inpatient residential treatment programs that totally deviate from the traditional disease approach discussed in chapter 2 are few and far between, however. Some of the traditional programs are incorporating parts of these new techniques into their overall program structure, but, for the most part, the fundamental disease framework of most inpatient residential programs remains. In chapter 7 we will tell you how to contact nearly all substance dependency treatment programs in the United States and help you locate the inpatient residential programs that are the least wedded to the traditional approach.

Innovations in Detoxification

Here we'll briefly overview several interesting developments in the area of detoxification. Detoxification is generally not thought of as treatment perse, but knowing about these developments will be helpful for you as you consider treatment options. These developments include rapid opiate detoxification, slow blind methadone detoxification, and some recent progress in the area of general detoxification methods.

Rapid Opiate Detoxification

Rapid opiate detoxification, a new approach to opiate dependence withdrawal, has recently received much attention from both the professional substance abuse literature and the popular press. Its developers report that it is a breakthrough technique that can be used to quickly detoxify persons addicted to heroin, methadone, or other powerful opiates. Essentially, it is a process whereby the opiate-dependent person is anesthetized and given naltrexone (discussed in chapter 6) to induce withdrawal while he or she is unconscious. In a sense, it is both a detoxification method and a treatment approach since clients are provided with naltrexone therapy and ongoing counseling upon release. While those who introduced this method make claims of high success in the use of this approach, the treatment community has yet to be convinced of its long-term efficacy. This rather costly approach is not widely available, but could become so if claims of its success hold up.

If rapid opiate detoxification does become accepted as an improved procedure, this method could dramatically motivate addicts to stop use of heroin and other powerful opiates. The harsh withdrawal syndrome traditionally associated with chronic use of these opiates has presented a major obstacle for those who might have wanted to quit. Rapid detoxification techniques may also soon become available for dependence on other drugs as well. Though we await the results of more clinical research on rapid opiate detoxification before we can recommend this approach, we feel obligated to make you aware of this technique.

Slow Blind Methadone Detoxification

Since its inception, traditional methadone detoxification has always been a relatively gradual process, with decreasing doses of the drug administered until the person is finally weaned off methadone completely. The process has generally been in the range of two to four weeks and longer, depending on the agency setting and the dosage. Slow blind methadone detoxification is a process that is protracted, and dose reduction comes in much smaller increments. Slow methadone detoxification uses a much smaller dosage than the typical 5 milligrams per reduction. An important part of this process is that doses of a placebo follow the last dose of methadone without informing the person of the change. The person remains on the placebo for a while before being told that he or she is no longer taking methadone. Several studies suggest that this method of detoxification renders better results than the traditional method.

Changes in General Detoxification

There are at least two improvements in the overall detoxification process. The first is that medications that aid the detoxification process have evolved over the years and their variety has expanded. Medical professionals have more access to a wider range of medications to assist the detoxification process than they had even ten years ago. Some medications that were used to treat dependence on one drug are now showing promise for aiding the detoxification process from other drugs. While it is not a major breakthrough, this improvement and expansion of available medications is important to note. The second development in this area is that detoxification is now being done more on an outpatient basis than ever before. Although this shift is driven mostly by cost-containment goals, a number of studies demonstrate the value of outpatient detoxification when the person's physical health status is not in danger. Having to enter an inpatient detoxification program can be a critical obstacle for many who might otherwise consider quitting.

Alternative Self-Help Groups

One of the more noticeable innovations for helping people overcome addiction is the rise in the number of alternative self-help groups. Some of these approaches are similar to those of 12-step groups in that they subscribe to the disease theory of addiction; others depart radically from this approach. Compared to AA, all of these alternatives share a relatively recent history since all were created within the last twenty-five years. Below we provide for you an overview of

each of them and give their website address. On their websites you will find a wide range of information about these
groups, including their purpose, whom they are intended to
serve, how to contact their headquarters, how to start
groups, and where established groups meet, including location and times. Most have chatrooms, with some even hold-
ing official meetings in on-line chatrooms. None of those we
mention below charge a fee for access to information on
their websites or attending face-to-face group meetings; like
12-step groups, these services are free.

Rational Recovery: www.rational.org/recovery

Rational Recovery (RR) was founded in 1985 by Jack
Trimpey, a clinical social worker. From that time until just
recently, Rational Recovery was fast becoming the largest
network of alternative self-help groups available for those
with substance dependency problems, filling an important
gap for those who found 12-step groups unappealing. Many
hundreds of meetings were available across the nation.
Much of the treatment community, including the criminal
justice system, had begun to recognize the potential value of
RR group participation for some of its clients. RR has recently concluded that recovery meetings are unnecessary to
overcome substance dependency, and participating in them
may actually exacerbate the situation. The organization has
now made a firm commitment no longer to offer recovery
meetings. Instead, it now offers training in what is referred

to as Addictive Voice Recognition Technique (AVRT), a cognitive-behavioral strategy that relies on changing one's thinking patterns and controlling one's motivations and is intended to provide all that is needed to overcome compulsions to use alcohol and other drugs when abstinence is the goal. Though many have expressed reservations about this move by RR and about the effectiveness of AVRT without group meetings, you will find numerous impressive testimonials about how this simple technique has radically changed the lives of some of those who have successfully applied it.

We include RR in this discussion of alternative self-help groups because it had become so widely known and used by so many over the last ten years. Additionally, many who have heard of RR as an alternative to 12-step groups have probably not realized that it has changed its helping strategy. We have not yet seen, and perhaps will never see, an official recommendation from RR about where those who want to attend meetings should go, but we suspect that SMART (discussed below) might be the place. Drawing heavily on the cognitive-behavioral work of Albert Ellis, both organizations continue to operate from similar philosophical and theoretical orientations.

Self Management and Recovery Training: www:smartrecovery.org

Self Management and Recovery Training (SMART) is a self-help organization that evolved from Rational Recovery.

SMART's philosophy is similar to that of 12-step groups in only one way: it is an abstinence-based program. However, it does not subscribe to the disease theory of substance dependence or the powerlessness belief inherent in the 12-steps. It does not draw on ideas from religion or require that its participants see themselves as alcoholics or addicts. Its philosophy and approach are grounded in the work of psychologist Albert Ellis and in cognitive-behavioral psychotherapy. SMART is a rapidly growing organization that now offers meetings in about two-thirds of the states. Meetings are also available in Canada, Australia, and Europe. Because of the position that RR has recently taken about recovery meetings, SMART might see the number of its groups expand rapidly in the near future. The purposes and methods of SMART can be found on their website and are as follows:

> We help individuals gain independence from addictive behavior.
> We teach how to:
>> A: enhance and maintain motivation to abstain
>> B: cope with urges
>> C: manage thoughts, feelings and behavior
>> D: balance momentary and enduring satisfactions
> Our efforts are based on scientific knowledge, and evolve as scientific knowledge evolves.
>
> Individuals who have gained independence from addictive behavior are invited to stay involved with us, to enhance their gains and help others.

Women For Sobriety: www.womenforsobriety.org

Women For Sobriety (WFS) is the oldest of the alternative self-help groups that we will discuss. It was founded by the late Dr. Jean Kirkpatrick in 1976 as a women's alternative to Alcoholics Anonymous. The organization is now open to women who are dependent on alcohol as well as other drugs. Dr. Kirkpatrick was a sociologist who had had a personal struggle with alcohol addiction for twenty-eight years. She attended AA meetings but found their authoritarian nature and chauvinistic views to be incompatible with her own unique needs as a woman. Furthermore, she often experienced a desire to drink after attending these meetings. WFS is based on thirteen statements that form the "New Life Program." These statements are grounded in various well-established theories, including cognitive-behavioral, feminist, and self-efficacy theory. They can be found on the WFS website and are listed below.

I have a life-threatening problem that once had me.
Negative thoughts destroy only myself.
Happiness is a habit I will develop.
Problems bother me only to the degree I permit them to.
I am what I think.
Life can be ordinary or it can be great.
Love can change the course of my world.
The fundamental object of life is emotional and spiritual growth.
The past is gone forever.

All love given returns.
Enthusiasm is my daily exercise.
I am a competent woman and have much to give life.
I am responsible for myself and for my actions.

Currently there are more than three hundred WFS meetings available in the United States, Canada, England, New Zealand, Australia, Ireland, and Finland. On-line meetings are also offered and conducted by WFS Coordinators.

Secular Organizations for Sobriety:
www.cfiwest.org/sos

Secular Organizations for Sobriety (SOS), also known as Save Our Selves, is a network of self-help groups for alcohol- and drug-dependent persons who are uncomfortable with the religious or spiritual content of 12-step groups. The organization was founded by James Christopher in 1986. Christopher began attending AA meetings in 1978 to help him deal with his alcohol dependence. He became extremely frustrated with the religious tone of AA meetings and created his own group in which such an emphasis was excluded. While SOS groups do not adhere to the powerless principle and hold positions on issues that are completely different from those held by 12-step groups, these groups are still more similar to 12-step groups than any of the others discussed in this chapter. They refer to their members as alcoholics and addicts, and they subscribe to the disease theory of substance dependence. Like the other alternative groups discussed, the number of groups has expanded over the years. Groups exist in about half of the states, and meetings are also held in Australia, Canada, and Europe. The General Principles of SOS presented on its website include:

All those who sincerely seek sobriety are welcome as members in any SOS group.

Although sobriety is an individual responsibility, life does not have to be faced alone. The support of other alcoholics and addicts is a vital adjunct to recovery. In SOS, members share experiences, insights, information, and supportive group meetings.

Sobriety is the number one priority in an alcoholic's or addict's life. As such, they must abstain from all drugs or alcohol.

SOS is not a spin-off of any religious group. There is no hidden agenda, as SOS is concerned with sobriety, not religiosity.

SOS seeks only to promote sobriety amongst those who suffer from alcoholism or other drug addictions. As a group, SOS has no opinion on outside matters and does not wish to become entangled in outside controversy.

To avoid unnecessary entanglements, each SOS group is self-supporting through contributions from its members, and refuses outside support.

Honest, clear, and direct communication of feelings, thoughts, and knowledge aids in recovery and in choosing non-destructive, non-delusional, and rational approaches to living sober and rewarding lives.

As knowledge of drinking or addiction might cause a person harm or embarrassment in the outside world, SOS guards the anonymity of its membership and the contents of its discussions from those not within the group.

SOS encourages the scientific study of alcoholism and addiction in all their aspects. SOS does not limit its outlook to one area of knowledge or theory of alcoholism and addiction.

When you retrieve material about SOS from the Internet, you might also consider looking up LifeRing Secular Recovery. This organization is among the network of groups that constitute SOS and has a very comprehensive, informative website. They even list a number of inpatient residential programs for consideration and state to what degree these programs incorporate 12-step meetings into their treatment approach. See www.unhooked.com.

Moderation Management: www.moderation.org

Moderation Management (MM) is a self-help group primarily for those who have experienced difficulty with alcohol abuse. The group's philosophy diverges radically from that of 12-step groups in many ways. MM does not subscribe to the disease theory of alcohol dependence or to the position that persons who have experienced problems with alcohol necessarily need to practice abstinence. Their position is that many people who have experienced problems managing their intake of alcohol can learn to reduce their drinking to nonproblematic levels. They clearly maintain, however, that this approach is not appropriate for all alcohol abusers; in fact, MM is not intended for those with long histories of chronic alcohol dependence. They suggest that those with this kind of history, or whose health has been severely compromised by alcohol use, or who otherwise represent very serious cases of alcohol dependence, would probably be poor candidates for MM. In fact, their target group might be better characterized as problem drinkers rather than those who are obviously alcohol dependent. Moderation Management's website offers chatrooms and on-line meetings. While not as pervasive as some of the other groups we have discussed, MM is expanding and groups now meet in about one quarter of all of the states and also in some parts of Canada.

Moderation Management is not without its critics. Many assert that offering reduced drinking rather than abstinence as a goal is a dangerous proposition that could hurl those with many years' abstinence into an abysmal cycle of uncontrolled drinking. Some say that MM appeals to a false hope that alcohol-dependent persons hold about their ability to drink again. Conversely, the principles of MM seem to comport with research and recent developments in the field of substance dependency treatment that suggest that large numbers of persons reduce their intake of alcohol to less problematic levels and that abstinence is an unnecessary goal for some.

It is important to note that any discussion of MM, particularly with those affiliated with the treatment community or 12-step groups, will lead to a mention of the unfortunate and tragic car accident involving MM's founder, Audrey Kishline. After leaving MM and returning to AA in January of 2000, Kishline was involved in a car accident in March of that year, where she was charged with killing two people while driving while intoxicated. Ms. Kishline has now changed her position on the value of MM. Some blame AA for her circumstances, others blame her earlier involvement with MM, still others suggest she, and she alone, is responsible for driving while drinking, and looking for blame elsewhere is misguided. Many who participate in MM have expressed deep regret about Ms. Kishline's situation, but assert that the principles of MM continue to benefit them in numerous ways and see no reason to abandon them because of this unfortunate incident. MM's nine steps toward moderation and balance as presented on their website include:

Attend meetings (local groups or on-line) and learn about the program of Moderation Management. Note: For those who do not want to go to support groups, this program can be followed without attending meetings.

Abstain from alcoholic beverages for 30 days and complete steps three through six during this time.

Examine how drinking has affected your life.

Write down your life priorities.

Take a look at how much, how often, and under what circumstances you used to drink.

Learn the MM guidelines and limits for moderate drinking. (This information is provided at meetings and in MM literature.)

Set moderate drinking limits and start weekly "small steps" toward positive lifestyle changes.

Review your progress and update your goals.

Continue to make positive lifestyle changes, help newcomers to the group, and attend meetings as needed for ongoing support.

No doubt there are other self-help groups available to substance-dependent persons in various communities, though they may not have received the same level of attention by the popular and professional literature as those above. In fact, we know of one group that exists that has no organizing structure, set of principles, or even an identifying name. This group has developed naturally and meets once a week for the sole purpose of helping the participants maintain their abstinence. We also see no reason why such groups could not be created by others who choose to do the same, and this alternative should be included as a possible option when discussing alternatives to 12-step groups.

Innovations in Outpatient Treatment

Although most of the innovative options for assisting persons with their substance dependency problems have come in the form of new self-help groups, there are also at least three interesting developments in the area of outpatient treatment worth including in this chapter. Rather than attempt the near impossible task of identifying the various programs and professional practitioners who are involved in these developments, we will provide an overview of these developments. Later, in chapter 7, we will offer suggestions about how to shop around for outpatient treatment that is less anchored to the traditional approach of substance dependency treatment.

Innovations in Private Practice

Today, if someone with an addiction problem wanted to access professional help that was not grounded in the disease perspective, he or she would best be served by seeking outpatient help from professionals in private practice. That does not mean that some psychologists, social workers, and other professionals do not subscribe to the disease theory of substance dependence, it only means that you can increase your chances of being introduced to a nontraditional perspective if you seek the services of these persons. Most of them have had training far beyond the somewhat narrow view of the disease theory of addiction. Many are able to draw on a wide range of perspectives that are generally required of them as part of their advanced professional education. Similarly, many are familiar with the major emerging research findings regarding the effectiveness of new as well as standard treatment approaches. They are also more likely to integrate some of these new ideas into their practice with substance-dependent clients.

For example, many of these professionals are likely to be familiar with studies that suggest that a cognitive-behavioral approach that aims to change negative patterns of thinking is more effective with certain kinds of clients than participation in 12-step groups. In fact, cognitive-behavioral theory is beginning to direct much of the practice of these professionals. Similarly, many others in private practice are anchoring their practice with substance-dependent clients on social learning theory, while others are emphasizing biopsychosocial models of substance dependency. Most of these theories about human behavior, including habitual use of alcohol and other drugs, have been subjected to research by the various disciplines of which these professionals are members. Again, the important point is that if you want something other than the traditional disease-based approaches, such as those that have been studied by researchers, your best chance of getting it is from professionals in private practice.

One caveat is in order regarding professionals such as psychologists and licensed clinical social workers. Note that we did not include psychiatrists in our examples of alternative approaches. Psychiatrists are trained as medical doctors who focus on identifying disease and treating it. And, while there are many psychiatrists who do not subscribe to the disease explanation of addiction and are keenly aware of many theories of human behavior, your chances of connecting with one who has a non-disease treatment orientation might be less than your chances with some of the other professionals. Furthermore, psychiatrists unfamiliar with treating substance dependency might be too quick to prescribe other drugs to treat addiction that might actually exacerbate the problem.

Rather than considering them as primary providers of treatment, we prefer to include psychiatrists as case consultants when mental health conditions seem to warrant psychotropic medications or when there are pressing questions about the severity of a client's compromised mental health state.

Assistance from the Internet

As we all have come to know, the Internet has dramatically changed the way we gather information about things that interest us. Even if you have no access to the Internet in your home, most local libraries provide such access to its patrons. The influence of the Internet is no less apparent when it comes to gathering information about the world of addiction treatment. Currently, the Internet offers a wealth of information about various treatment options and many other aspects of alcohol and drug use. All of the new self-help groups identified earlier in this chapter have websites, and their services are free. Though there are many other forms of free assistance, many treatment-related services can be purchased on-line. The services an organization offers may range from a brief presentation of educational materials provided online, to counseling sessions set up on-line and conducted by phone. Many of these organizations offer the same kind of innovative assistance with regard to substance abuse problems as the new self-help groups discussed above. Below, we will discuss three examples of such on-line services and include their website addresses. A thorough search on the Internet will yield many more such websites.

Drinkwise: www.med.umich.edu/drinkwise

Drinkwise is a confidential, brief-intervention program for those with mild to moderate alcohol problems. The program is not designed for those with severe or chronic alcohol dependency or who otherwise might require more intensive treatment. Drinkwise encourages the user to decide whether he or she wants to reduce his or her drinking or quit altogether, then assists with reaching that goal. Drinkwise also offers a program for those who have been arrested for driving while under the influence of alcohol. In this program the client is directed to one of two formats with an emphasis on drinking and driving.

Addiction Alternatives: www.addictionalternatives.com

Addiction Alternatives is an alternative to traditional treatment and 12-step groups. Its founder and director is Marc Fern, a clinical psychologist with many years of personal and professional-practice experience with drugs. Drawing on both of these experiences, his practice with clients is grounded in the philosophy that people can learn how to overcome substance dependency and move on to enjoy life without practicing complete abstinence. His position is that some can use alcohol moderately and responsibly.

Behavior Therapy Associates:
www.behaviortherapy.com

Behavior Therapy Associates is an organization of psychologists providing clinical services, research, and training for health care and mental health providers. It also provides these services to organizations. One of its primary research and training interests is substance misuse. Its software programs teach how to moderate one's drinking, and its website provides a list of therapists across the United States who practice moderation training.

Wider Range of Outpatient Programs

As stated in chapter 2, for better or worse, outpatient treatment services for substance dependency have grown rapidly in recent years. A number of factors have contributed to this increase in outpatient services, notably cost containment efforts by Managed Care Organizations (MCOs) and growing recognition that the more expensive and intrusive inpatient residential care may not be necessary for many substance abusers. While many practitioners have become extremely frustrated by this movement driven by profit motives, some outpatient programs are experimenting with creative program planning that could prove beneficial to its clients. Drop-in activities, day treatment, evening treatment, and other kinds of programming offer different kinds of opportunities than the once-a-week counseling sessions typically provided a few years ago. On the one hand, we share the frustration of practitioners with the MCOs; on the other, as a potential consumer of outpatient services it is important for you to know that the variety of outpatient services in some communities are worth considering. Some of the more comprehensive day and evening outpatient programs have as many educational and/or therapeutic activities as some of the more relaxed inpatient residential programs.

Conclusion

Our overview of emerging alternatives and promising innovations in the area of addiction treatment is not presented as an indictment against traditional treatment or participation in 12-step groups. Indeed, many persons in this country have benefited from such treatment and from affiliating with 12-step groups. However, the unfortunate reality is that these programs have limited success. Although there are numerous reasons why they fail, the principle reason is that these approaches rely on a disease-based theory of addiction to the exclusion of other possible causes. The result of this unitary and often inflexible approach has essentially limited the menu of choices available to substance-dependent persons. The new strategies for overcoming addiction discussed in this chapter are a move from this impasse to more choices that might be more attractive and yield better results in certain types of persons. Yet, there is still much to be done; most of the new approaches that require face-to-face contact are still available only in certain parts of the country and in large metropolitan areas.

CHAPTER 6

The Environment of Addiction and Resolution

While the pharmacological properties of alcohol and various other drugs play an important role in addiction, use that results in dependence is heavily influenced by one's unique set of personal characteristics and environmental circumstances. Age, gender, socioeconomic status, mental health status, and a range of other conditions are all factors that converge with use and potential dependency. Similarly, these same factors can have a major influence in determining an appropriate course of intervention, a strategy that will have a higher probability of succeeding than other strategies. This chapter will identify the personal and environmental factors as well as drug-specific considerations that warrant attention as one contemplates recovery.

Personal and Environmental Factors

Severity of Problem

Severity of the problem could be the single most important factor in determining what kind of action needs to be taken. If you are considering doing something about your use of substances, you probably have some indication of the severity of your problems.

Treatment providers conduct various kinds of assessments with substance abusers to determine their degree of severity. Such assessments typically take the form of questionnaires that are completed through face-to-face interviews between the problem user and agency staff. These assessments generally include questions that pertain to the type and extent of use and to what degree use is affecting other areas of one's life, such as work, family, relationships, health, and the like. Before initiating agency-based recovery efforts, there are two important issues around agency-based assessments that you should consider. The first is that the accuracy of an assessment for severity of the problem very much depends on the honesty of the substance user during the assessment process. Many persons underreport the extent of their use and related problems. Second, some assessments can be self-serving for the agency where the process is taking place; the severity of use may be determined at a level that meets the requirement for admission to the program where the assessment happens to be done. If you feel that you need a professional assessment and have resources to do so, we recommend an independent assessment with a treatment professional in private practice. Let the practitioner know that you are primarily interested in an independent assessment. In many cases, a comprehensive and accurate assessment will take more than one session. If you do not have the resources for an independent assessment, talk with the staff at the agency you select so they can address any concerns you may have about the process.

Regardless of how severity is determined, it is the factor that will most dictate the course of appropriate intervention. Treatment can be conceptualized as being on a continuum from least intrusive to most intrusive, with least intrusive including such strategies as educational sessions or what is referred to as brief interventions and what we refer to in the second half of this book as "natural recovery." On the other end of the continuum exist long-term residential programs, including therapeutic communities. This continuum of options would also include self-help group; 12-step groups, as well as the alternatives to 12-step groups discussed in chapter 5.

Level of Motivation

Just as severity of the problem is the most important consideration when deciding what course of action needs to be taken, the level of one's motivation to change can be one of the best predictors of success. Being motivated to change can be especially difficult for persons who reap precious benefits from using and see little reward in stopping. Those who derive significant meaning in life, escape harsh physical and emotional realities, and others who meet important human needs through substance use will likely find stopping especially unappealing.

While it would be ideal for a person's level of motivation to be exceptionally high, this is generally not the case, nor does it have to be. The truth is that for nearly all there is some degree of ambivalence at the outset. However, for change to occur, the seeds of motivation must be present, where ambivalence can gradually be supplanted with resolve. Many persons enter and complete some of the most comprehensive inpatient residential treatments available, but make little progress toward quitting because the desire to do so simply is not there or is not cultivated.

If you are the person in need of help, you know how much you want and do not want to change. If you are assisting someone else, determining their level of motivation to quit can be difficult; many persons will say that they want to change but, deep down, they really do not. You can get a sense of one's level of motivation simply by being alert to behaviors that are consistent or inconsistent with someone wanting to change. For example, if the person you are assisting initiates discussions about changing or follows through on suggestions made about beginning the process, chances are that he or she really does want to change. On the other hand, if the person avoids such discussions or does not respond to advice, the level of motivation is likely to be much lower.

Treatment programs vary in the amount of attention they give to a client's level of motivation. However, regardless of the path out of addiction that is taken—be it treatment, self-help groups, or self-resolution—the importance of wishing to alter one's relationship with substances cannot be overstated.

Gender

Gender is also an important consideration for determining an appropriate course of intervention. While there are a number of commonalities between how men and women experience chronic use of alcohol and other drugs, there are also a number of distinct differences that should be understood. For example, the physiological damage that is often associated with long-term use occurs more rapidly with women and is also generally more severe. Because of the different expectations that our society holds of women, there can be an enormous amount of shame and guilt that women shoulder because of heavy use. Women who become entangled in the street subculture of illicit drugs like heroin and crack cocaine use can encounter traumatic and demeaning experiences trying to maintain their habits. And, of course, women with children have specific needs to consider as they think about treatment. Because of these and a host of other gender-specific factors, providers must approach treatment of women and men differently.

It is only recently that the treatment community has begun to give serious attention to these differences and to shape their programming in response. Unfortunately, this response has been slow and in some places is even nonexistent.

There are too few treatment slots for addicted women with children. Too often, programs still continue to rely on approaches designed for men, or they use insensitive, counterproductive techniques inappropriate for women's unique treatment needs. Some women also find the leadership, structure, and philosophy of 12-step groups inappropriate for them, given their past experiences and feelings about what transpired in their lives during periods of heavy alcohol and drug use. When exploring treatment options for women, be sure that these and other unique issues that confront them are given special attention by the treatment program under consideration.

Age

While age might be seen as a rather obvious factor that should be thought about when deciding what to do about a serious alcohol or drug problem, an inordinate number of treatment programs are designed for adolescents that essentially model their activities after adult programs. It is also not unusual in adult programs to have nineteen- and twenty-year-olds in group therapy sessions or in 12-step meetings with persons in their fifties and sixties. Many of these programs are unrealistic and perhaps even dangerous for young people. Age and age variability are important factors that are given different levels of attention across different programs.

Because of what is known about biopsychosocial development among humans and the related challenges that exist across the life span, we know that there are striking differences between the treatment needs of adolescents, adults, and older adults. For example, there might not be much difference between the treatment needs of, say, a thirty-five-year-old and thirty-nine-year-old; however, there is a critical difference between the treatment needs of a fifteen- and a nineteen-year-old. Similarly, in some cases substance-using behaviors of adolescents, particularly alcohol and marijuana experimentation, may indicate a potential problem; yet, it might also be attributed to normal developmental processes that the individual will outgrow naturally after some time.

At the other end of the continuum, the fact that older adults tend to metabolize alcohol and other drugs at a much slower rate than the young could indicate different levels of physical damage with the same amount of use. Many of these older individuals also develop problems with substances after significant losses in their lives, including retirement, whereas, younger persons tend to use and subsequently run into difficulty with substance misuse for different reasons. The key point here is that although age might appear to be an obvious factor that treatment programs consider when developing their treatment activities, attention to age-specific demands may or may not exist within a program. If the person seeking help is young or substantially older than others in a particular program under consideration, by sure that treatment responds to his or her age-related needs. Additionally, as a rule, we suggest that adolescents not be placed in programs that primarily treat adults.

Ethnicity

Ethnicity is an another important consideration for sub-stance-dependent persons seeking help because one's ethnic-ity in the United States is such a critical element of who a person is. Ethnicity plays a major role in determining one's values, beliefs, and behaviors. Yet the importance of ethnic-ity in determining an appropriate course of action for alco-hol- and drug-dependent persons has received little attention from researchers. The little research that has been done in the area has not resulted in broad-base changes within the treatment community.

Given this state of affairs, here are a few things to con-sider, particularly if you are a member of an ethnic minor-ity group. Addiction treatment in the United States as an enterprise emerged with white males as its primary client base. Alcoholics Anonymous, the template of all 12-step groups, also began with a similar orientation. While both treatment and 12-step programs have served many women as well as people from various ethnic backgrounds, most have done so and continue to do so from a white-male worldview of reality. This orientation is not one that con-tinues out of malice or even insensitivity to the needs of members of other groups. The challenge of operating from a more multicultural framework (a much more compli-cated task) is often too complex and overwhelming for the ordinary treatment agency to meet.

If you or the person needing help is a member of an eth-nic minority group, it is important to know that the world of treatment is confronted with the same kinds of challenges around race faced by the larger society. The different realities that emanate from distinct norms and customs that members of these groups bring to treatment can be very difficult for treatment providers to understand and value. Some programs are experimenting with culturally specific interventions, but most have not responded to the unique needs of African Americans, Hispanic Americans, or Native Americans, for example.

There are some treatment programs that specifically cater to various groups and utilize culturally specific interventions, but such programs, like other innovative programs, are not widely accessible. As is the case with alternative self-help groups, what little is available is likely to be in large urban areas. If you or the person seeking help is a member of an ethnic minority group and seeking help from an organization that typically does not serve that group, ask its treatment staff about their ability and limitations to respond to such ethnic difference. While the subject of ethnicity is not widely discussed by treatment providers or in recovery meetings, it is one that we see important enough to bring to your attention.

Employment Status

Very often, substance misuse interrupts employment or at least adversely affects it in important ways. Persons may lose jobs, quit jobs, or have their employment threatened if something is not done about their substance abuse problem. Even when job performance is not severely compromised by one's substance misuse, many persons employ quitting strategies such as geographic relocation or entering treatment that necessitate quitting their jobs. Most persons planning to do something about their addiction, particularly if the choice is formal treatment, will need to consider how to manage their job situation. Should they reveal to their employer what their plans are? Will they need to take a leave of absence, and is that possible? Can they undergo treatment and simultaneously keep their jobs? Can they work on a reduced schedule to accommodate treatment requirements? How will undergoing treatment affect their job and how will they be perceived by others upon completion of treatment? These and a number of other questions may need to be pondered by those in the workforce who plan to enter treatment.

At the other end of the spectrum, there are persons who are substance dependent but unemployed or only marginally employed. Employment is generally more of a concern for them once they complete treatment. One of the major risk factors for such persons returning to substance misuse is the idle time that comes with being out of work. Some treatment programs do a pretty good job of connecting clients with community resources to respond to their clients' various employment needs, while others do not.

Whether one has stable employment, sufficient education or vocational skills to secure employment, or whether one is barely employable, another factor to consider around employment relates to the meaningfulness of the work one does. People who return from treatment to a boring job might find their cessation efforts threatened by monotonous, unfulfilling work. While most people's lives would probably improve if their jobs were more fulfilling, this fact is particularly important to consider for those who have lived in the world of alcohol and drug addiction. So, as you plan a course of action, consider the implications of employment-related issues and how they might influence your decision about what to do.

Education

One's level of education is very much related to one's employability and the capacity to maintain employment options. However, the role of education in determining an appropriate course of intervention for a substance misuse problem is often overlooked. Some approaches to addiction employ strategies that require certain levels of literacy in order to participate and complete their program. Some brief interventions and programs that utilize information sharing in the form of reading materials require a minimum level of literacy. Introspective types of psychotherapy that rely heavily on one's mastery of language to express feelings tend to have better success with those who have higher levels of education.

On the other side of the coin, some treatment programs over-rely on simple canned techniques that do not adequately engage those accustomed to more complex ideas. Many long-term residential programs, particularly therapeutic communities, utilize much of the language of the streets to communicate educational and therapeutic subject matter to their clients. Professional persons or others with high levels of education might find use of this type of language to convey treatment concepts problematic, and even offensive.

While many highly trained professionals are employed in treatment settings, the bulk of the staff often consists of persons "in recovery." Some of them also have advanced educational credentials, though many do not. For the well-educated person who may be paying thousands of dollars for treatment, such differentials can be troubling.

Health Status

The deleterious impact of addiction on the health of some users can be an extremely serious matter. Persons develop problems with substance abuse by medicating illness and injury as well as the emotional difficulties they experience. People also develop health problems that are a result of their chronic use of alcohol and other drugs. Many people with long-standing dependencies develop a range of health problems, some quite serious. While there is a great deal of public awareness about the relationship between HIV through needle sharing and unsafe sexual practices, most persons are probably oblivious to the current epidemic of hepatitis C and the increase in other serious blood-borne diseases.

Most persons are even unaware of the health problems associated with long-term use of common legal drugs like alcohol. For example, chronic use of alcohol can result in a host of health problems that range from the mild to the acute and include such conditions as high blood pressure, ulcers, pancreatitis, and cirrhosis of the liver. In fact, many are referred to treatment facilities by health-care professionals who see them in emergency rooms and hospitals for a variety of illnesses and injuries. Not all, but many persons with extensive histories of substance abuse have neglected their dental hygiene to the point that they have also developed serious dental-related problems that require medical care. Not to be ignored in any discussion about health and substance abuse is the high rate of coexisting tobacco dependence among substance abusers. Health-related problems from tobacco use results in about half a million deaths a year in the United States.

Some treatment programs do a better job than others with problem users who require medical attention. Some facilities actually have medical professionals on staff and on site. However, many other facilities are not equipped to handle persons with even mild health problems or those that require only minimal medical attention. Also to be considered is that standard activities in some programs require a level of mobility and health to fully take advantage of what a program offers. Those that include strenuous physical exercise as an integral part of their treatment would be such an example.

In Part Two of this book, where we discuss strategies for recovery without treatment, we suggest that persons who plan such an approach first get a thorough physical examination before proceeding. Such an examination will dictate what can and cannot be considered as cessation strategies. The same holds true for those leaning toward formal treatment. Certain health-related conditions can have a great deal of influence on what treatment options should and should not be considered. And, if the facility does not offer a comprehensive physical examination as part of its treatment, the person needing help should secure this service independently.

Mental Health Status

Concerns about mental health are similar to those about physical health and can be a critical element in a substance dependency situation. People can develop problems with substances because of compromised mental health and, conversely, mental health problems can be the result of excessive substance abuse. There is a good amount of research that suggests that preexisting mental health disorders play a major role in problematic use of alcohol and other drugs and some patients become habituated to using them. Some studies suggest that an alarming percentage of women who use street drugs such as heroin and cocaine are victims of sexual and physical abuse. The unfortunate reality is that mental health problems can impair your ability to employ strategies that will help you quit even when the desire to stop is sincere.

Use of certain types of drugs, particularly for long periods of time and in large quantities, can put one at risk for serious mental health problems. For example, chronic use of some hallucinogens may result in anxiety disorders and severe psychoses. Extended years of heavy alcohol use can lead to permanent loss of memory and severe brain damage. The toxic compounds in aerosol sprays, glue, gasoline, and other volatile substances that constitute the inhalants can lead to brain damage.

Mental health difficulties among problem users represent a tremendous challenge for treatment professionals. As in the case of medical examinations, some programs provide thorough mental health assessments as part of their treatment. However, simply conducting a mental health assessment does not necessarily mean that an appropriate course of mental health treatment will follow, or if its does, that it will be effective. Unfortunately, some mental health disorders can baffle even highly trained professionals with years of experience.

Although there is still much to be done, at least now there are programs designed specifically to address coexisting mental health and substance abuse problems. Often referred to as dual diagnosis programs, and becoming more widely available in most areas, they represent an attempt to respond to the complex issue of mental health and substance abuse. Substance abusers with discernible mental health problems should explore such treatment. Where dual diagnosis programs are not available, the staff will need to coordinate appropriate mental health services.

In terms of compromised mental health, also be advised that those with active severe mental health disorders will likely be poor candidates for self-help group participation. Also know that withdrawal from or quitting long-term use of most mind-altering drugs typically produces uncomfortable emotional states such as depression, anxiety, agitation, poor concentration, and the like. Do not confuse these temporary states with permanent mental health disorders. This kind of naturally occurring uneasiness eventually fades. Of course, if such conditions persist, more serious mental health problems could be present.

Resources

Just as the severity of the problem may be one of the most critical factors that determine what *should* be done, the level of one's resources will be the major factor that determines what *can* be done. After reading this book, and perhaps after consulting others, you may decide that the best course of action would be to enroll in a particular form of treatment. Similarly, you may also decide that entering formal treatment at this time would be an ill-advised choice and that self-recovery is a more promising path to pursue. Your ability to fully implement either of these alternatives will depend on whether or not you have the resources to do so.

The kinds of resources that may be required in these situations are of three principal types: (1) resources to pay for the type of strategy decided upon, (2) various personal characteristics that can be seen as resources, and (3) social resources needed to support a change effort. Even when persons choose self-recovery, our research has shown that these three kinds of resources play a pivotal role in one's ability to successfully overcome serious problems with alcohol and other drugs. Chief among the first type of resource mentioned is money—plain and simple—or other financial assets that can be quickly converted to it. Money may be needed to pay for the special kind of services that you have determined will give you the best chance of getting desired results. In a real sense, insurance or managed care coverage represent money for treatment. However, such treatment may not be covered or it may only be partially covered.

Good examples of personal characteristics that can be important resources include physical health, mental health, level of education, and employability. These can serve as critical assets that go a long way toward increasing the probability of success.

A more intangible resource, yet one no less important, is social support. This kind of support may come from significant others, family, friends, and, very often, coworkers. For people in treatment, support from these important persons is an essential ingredient for success. Sometimes, substance-dependent persons have become so estranged from family and others who could provide valuable social support that it is difficult to draw upon them as resources. In other cases, significant others, family, and friends are so entangled in substance abuse themselves that they represent deficit relationships rather than assets that can help the process to quit.

Irrespective of what your choice for change is, these resources, or lack of them, will determine which options are available to you and which are not.

Social-Environmental Factors

Closely related to the social supports discussed above are social environmental conditions within which the substance-using person lives. As discussed elsewhere in this book, those whose lives have become completely immersed in the street drug subculture, with its attendant criminal activity, violence, and deviant lifestyle, have a different kind of challenge than those who are able to successfully straddle both the conventional and the drug-using world. Those who live in and are able to continue to function reasonably well in an environment that does not condone heavy substance use have a distinct advantage over those who do not. Persons who live in communities where heavy alcohol use and illicit drug use are integral pieces of the fabric of the community may face more difficulty than those from neighborhoods where such activities are largely absent. Those who have been in and out of prison because of drug-related activity, will have different obstacles to overcome from those who have never been incarcerated.

Whether or not someone is a parent and how he or she is able to manage parental responsibilities is an important consideration. Is the person an active or inactive member of a church, synagogue, mosque, or other faith-based organizations? Is he or she enrolled in school? Is he or she involved in hobbies or activities beyond those associated with alcohol and drug use? Does his or her social network consist of using as well as non-using friends, and how close is his or her connection with each? To what extent does use of alcohol or other drugs play an active role in his or her daily life? Is the person at risk for physical abuse or other dangers? These are only a few of the considerations you need to make regarding the user's social environmental conditions before taking an appropriate course of action.

Types of Drugs Used

Mind-altering drugs of abuse are often classified into five or more categories, according to their pharmacological similarities. Drugs within these various categories affect people in very different ways and require different considerations when problems develop from using them. Some of these drugs do not fit neatly into one specific group, while others could be classified into more than one category. For example, heroin, alcohol, and nicotine can have both stimulating as well as sedating effects on the user. Below, we identify these major categories of drugs, give a brief description of their effects, and point out some of the key issues a person should consider when persuing change.

Depressants

Depressants (also referred to as sedative-hypnotics) tend to depress the central nervous system and induce drowsiness. They include alcohol, barbiturates, mild tranquilizers, and other drugs that produce sedating effects. One of the principle concerns about the most frequently used drug in this category, alcohol, is that it is a legal drug and widely available to the adult public. This easy access presents a unique challenge for society and for those who want to quit. Many of the other drugs in this category are also obtained legally through prescriptions from health-care providers. Because of the legal status of these drugs, the severity of dependency can be underestimated. Abrupt withdrawal from large quantities of depressants can pose serious risks for seizures, comas, and, in some cases, even death. Although many people gradually wean themselves off these drugs, we recommend medically supervised detoxification for chronic users or for those taking large quantities of drugs in this category. In most communities there are generally public as well as private detoxification centers. Many are connected with hospitals and most are listed in the Yellow Pages of phone directories.

Stimulants

Stimulants include amphetamines, methamphetamines, powder and "crack" cocaine, and many other drugs referred to as "speed." These drugs increase energy, alertness, and motor activity. The caffeine in coffee and soft drinks is one of the milder forms of these drugs. One of the main concerns here is that obtaining drugs like cocaine and crack cocaine puts one into contact with the more dangerous world and the deviant values of the drug subculture. The more attached one becomes to that culture and the more disconnected from normal activities, the more difficult it can be to return to conventional life. Additionally, some of these substances are taken intravenously, thus suggesting possible exposure to blood-borne diseases like HIV and hepatitis through needle sharing.

Although it is not life threatening, withdrawal from powerful stimulants can result in extended periods of depression and lethargy. Many people return to using them simply to eliminate these unpleasant states. Persons who are at the initial stage of overcoming dependence on stimulants must realize that while these states can be somewhat protracted, they are temporary and will pass with time. Those who plan to undergo treatment for stimulant dependence should expect treatment providers to respond to the implications of these extended conditions and be able to demonstrate an ability to effectively address them.

Opiates

Opiates (also referred to as narcotics) include drugs such as opium, heroin, morphine, methadone, codeine, and a range of other natural and synthetic substances with opiate-like properties. Opiates are commonly used for the relief and management of pain. While opiates like heroin are generally purchased "on the streets," one can legally obtain opiates by getting a prescription from a health-care professional; in some states, milder opiates can be found in over-the-counter medications. Like other classes of drugs, opiates can have both a sedating as well as a stimulating effect on the user. The same concerns that apply to illicit opiates like heroin also apply to cocaine; that is, regular use can put one at risk for contact with and immersion into the dangerous street subculture. And, while there has been an increase in sniffing or "snorting" and smoking heroin, particularly among the middle class, the principle mode of administration of the drug continues to be intravenous injection; hence, the increased risk of contracting diseases. An additional concern about use of powerful opiates is related to the very uncomfortable withdrawal symptoms experienced when someone tries to withdraw. While this discomfort is generally not dangerous, it can easily lead to resumed use, even when the intent to stop is genuine.

One of the most popular and widely available forms of treatment for opiate dependence is methadone maintenance. We caution against entering a methadone maintenance program too quickly. Methadone is a powerful, relatively long-acting synthetic opiate whose substitution for less potent opiates like heroin can lead to other problems, notably an extreme addiction to methadone. In some cases, dependence on heroin and other opiates is so severe that methadone maintenance is justified; however, in other cases, this substitution of addictions is not warranted. Three to four days of flulike symptoms from heroin withdrawal is a minor imposition when contrasted to several weeks of discomfort that can be associated with methadone withdrawal. Additionally, methadone maintenance programs can increase one's exposure to and acquaintances with others who use opiates like heroin, a situation that can hold its own potential risks for someone trying to quit.

Hallucinogens

Hallucinogens include LSD, psilocybin, mescaline, PCP, and other drugs that alter visual and auditory perception. Reality and ordinary images may be mildly or grossly distorted when using these drugs. Hallucinogens can be found in various kinds of plants or can be produced synthetically. An episode of use is often referred to as "trip," suggesting a departure from reality. Although consumption of many of these drugs had decreased from their introduction in the mid to late sixties, there has been a discernible rise in their use in recent years among young people. Because of the powerful influence on consciousness produced by these drugs, use can sometimes produce panic attacks, psychotic reactions, and unpredictably hazardous behavior. Flashbacks may occur weeks and even months after use. Since there is no physical dependence that develops with most hallucinogens, detoxification is generally not required. The fact that many traditional programs tend to operate from the perspective that the client needs to demonstrate physical dependence is an important consideration in such cases and will likely preclude admission to most treatment programs. Without major adjustments to accommodate the unique situation of most hallucinogen users, conventional treatment or participation in 12-step groups can be of limited value.

Often the motivation to stop using these unpredictable substances is preceded by a "bad trip" or other negative experiences produced by the drug. While hallucinogen use can be very hazardous, it tends to be associated with youth, and use generally diminishes with age. Formal treatment for hallucinogen use is likely to be more appropriate for PCP or angel dust than for the other substances in this category. If formal assistance is needed, we suggest you seek someone in private practice who has experience with working with youth and hallucinogen users.

Cannabis

Cannabis refers to marijuana and hashish. These substances have also been referred to as hallucinogens. While the sensory changes associated with the hallucinogens discussed above can be present with marijuana and hashish use, such alterations are typically milder. The euphoric effects of these drugs can include relaxation, enhanced sense of sight and sound, and an altered sense of time. Some users have reported paranoia and, to a lesser extent, panic attacks. Like most hallucinogens, cannabis use does not produce physical dependence for most. Similarly, the absence of physical dependence presents a challenge for the treatment community, with some providers only offering assistance for the most chronic cases of cannabis use or not offering treatment at all. Because casual nonproblematic use of marijuana is so widespread, both treatment providers and the general public often question the necessity of treatment.

Although marijuana is one of the most popular drugs, it is the one that is least understood. Like alcohol, many persons use the drug on occasion with no difficulty, while some, though significantly fewer, become chronic heavy users who actually experience discernible protracted withdrawal symptoms when they stop. Though treatment for marijuana use has typically been the province of adolescent programs, the increased potency of the drug has created concern in adult programs. Treatment that goes beyond a simple educational approach tends to be of the traditional disease type discussed in chapter 2 where persons are encouraged to attend Narcotics Anonymous meetings during and after treatment. We see little rationale for approaching "pot smoking" in this fashion and encourage those who think that they need help to seek someone in private practice who has a deep understanding of marijuana use and a reasonable record of success with clients.

Inhalants

Inhalants include a group of volatile chemicals that can be found in products such as glue, gasoline, aerosol paints, cleaning agents, and other toxic substances. Typically, the fumes from these substances are inhaled by the user and produce a euphoria similar to the effects of alcohol, including intoxication, reduced inhibitions, slurred speech, excitement, and a sense of floating, for example. These effects are of short duration, generally lasting between 15 and 45 minutes. While some adults use inhalants, most use occurs among teens. Inhaling these highly toxic substances has been found to be especially risky. Depending on the substance used as well as the duration of use, inhalant use has been found to be directly linked to a wide range of deleterious physical and mental conditions, including permanent brain damage. Because of widespread use among the young, treatment for inhalant use often occurs at programs that treat adolescents. Those who are contemplating adolescent treatment should be clear that the specific program they are considering is geared especially to unique adolescent developmental needs and is not a mirror of an adult program.

Because of the high risk of brain damage from inhalant use, we encourage parents to seek assistance for their children as soon as possible. If your child's clothing smells like glue, gasoline, or solvents there might be cause for immediate action. Irreversible brain damage is substantially higher for those who have used for long periods of time than for those who are just experimenting. We suggest complete mental health and neurological examinations followed by inpatient monitoring to determine mental health stability.

Club Drugs

Club Drugs include MDMA (ecstasy), Ketamine (special K), and a range of other drugs in various categories that are sometimes used at all-night dance parties (raves), dance clubs, and bars by young people. Ecstasy has recently received considerable attention from the public media. Both ecstasy and Ketamine can have hallucinogenic effects on the user; however, ecstasy will also produce stimulating effects, whereas Ketamine produces more dreamlike states. Some of the other club drugs such as Gamma-hydroxybutyrate (GHB) and Rohypnol (roofies) have sedating effects. Use of Gamma-hydroxybutyrate and Rohypnol have been implicated in some "date rapes." While there is disagreement about the harmful effects of MDMA, the more popular of these club drugs, reported increase in its use has prompted concern from the National Institute on Drug Abuse. Again, as is the case of treatment for abuse of other substances among the young, these can be very challenging cases to deal with, particularly when many users feel that the negative consequences of taking some of these drugs are minor or nonexistent.

Because of the range of pharmacological effects of these various club drugs, it is inappropriate to pursue similar kinds of treatment for all users. We do recommend, however, that you consider the unique effects of different types of these drugs on the user if you are seeking help for yourself or someone else. For example, those who are chronically using a club drug that produces a powerful sedating effect should be mindful of our discussion on depressants and heed our cautions.

The categories of the drugs above probably include those with which you or the person you are assisting is having trouble. While all mind-altering substances have similar qualities, there can be distinct differences in the way they affect people in use and dependency. These differences can have important implications as one begins to think about an appropriate course of intervention. For example, drugs in some of the categories identified above do not produce physical dependence, yet most treatment programs are designed to respond to the needs of those who are both physically and psychologically dependent on drugs. Below we highlight other important considerations that are specific to the actual act of using these substances.

Use Patterns

Thus far in this chapter, we have discussed how personal characteristics, environmental conditions, and use of different types of drugs are important factors to consider when planning a course of intervention for yourself or someone you care about. In this section we discuss how certain patterns of using these substances can also influence your decision about what to do. We give brief attention to three essential areas: how the drug is taken, the amount of use, and the level of involvement in the drug subculture.

How the Drug Is Taken

The way in which a person takes a drug plays an important role in determining the pharmacological action of the substance on the body and, hence, how it is experienced by the user. It determines how fast and how much of the drug will reach the brain and the level of concentration it will have there. Similarly, the method of administration plays an important role in determining how quickly the substance is metabolized by the body and then leaves it. These factors come together to create the level of reinforcing properties, both physical and mental, that the substance holds for the user. The method in which drugs are taken may also indicate one's level of involvement with the drug and possibly the street subculture—all factors that can determine the severity of problem.

Of the popular methods of taking drugs, injecting them into the bloodstream is the quickest and most efficient way to get them to the brain in a concentrated form. It is also the most dangerous, since adverse affects are difficult to correct once the drug is injected. Swallowing drugs is the slowest and least efficient method. Inhaling is a relatively quick method but not as efficient as injecting. Many persons now smoke drugs other than marijuana, notably crack cocaine. Smoking is an inhalation method that produces quick results for drugs that can be used that way.

If you or the person your are attempting to help are regularly injecting drugs, chances are that you or that person has a fairly serious problem or will soon have one if injection continues. Indeed, many who swallow or inhale drugs often start injecting during the later stages of their addictions. While some people inject drugs without difficulty, most develop severe problems and require intrusive strategies to quit. The same applies to those who smoke crack cocaine—another difficult situation to reverse without extensive effort. Conversely, swallowing drugs can lead to dependency, but the reinforcing properties of swallowing are not as strong as those associated with injecting or inhaling. Of course, this does not mean that persons who swallow drugs do not experience serious cases of addiction (one need only recall the image of someone severely dependent on alcohol to know that this is not true), it simply suggests that those who inject or smoke drugs might develop more severe problems quicker.

Extent of Use

How much, how often, and how long one has used alcohol and other drugs are also important to consider when attempting to determine the level of severity and how to proceed. Generally, frequent and extensive use of large amounts of most of the drugs discussed above will result in more severe dependency and related problems. This kind of problem user may benefit from more intrusive intervention, although more treatment does not naturally follow from heavier use. For those whose use is less extensive, less intrusive types of treatment should always be the first option. While one might see the relationship between the extent of use and the severity of the problem as simple common sense, surprisingly such distinctions are not given much attention by some treatment providers.

Chronic and extremely high levels of use may also necessitate close monitoring during detoxification from drugs that would not ordinarily require it. For example, while detoxification from opiates is generally not life threatening, it is wise to monitor those who are withdrawing from very high doses of methadone, particularly if the detoxification period is of short duration.

Level of Involvement in Drug Subculture

While this discussion can apply to those who take drugs such as alcohol and prescription medications that are obtained through legal channels, it applies more to those who use illicit drugs such as heroin, cocaine, and crack cocaine. As suggested earlier in this chapter, as persons become more involved in illicit drugs and more dependent on their use, they often drift from conventional relationships. Their friends and friendship network-change, their hangouts change, and their recreational activities are replaced with behaviors related to drug seeking, purchasing, and using. As they become deeper involved in these activities, these conventional relationships deteriorate while the drug-using circles and activities expand.

Persons with severe drug problems often become immersed in the street subculture to the point that conventional relationships and even conventional roles disappear. Some become completely estranged from family, quit or lose their jobs, and survive by becoming involved in the underground economy of drug dealing and street crimes. When this level of involvement exists, the problem is generally severe and the kind of life changes required will be extensive. This is especially true for those who have been involved in this underground drug world for many years. Conversely, a person who is using cocaine daily but still maintaining family and conventional relationships and managing daily responsibilities would likely benefit from a different, perhaps less intrusive, form of intervention.

Conclusion

As you can see, there is a wide range of personal, environmental, and drug-use characteristics that you should consider as you contemplate a course of action for yourself or someone you care about. While we have included those that we think are the most important to take into account, there are, no doubt, many other characteristics that may be equally important for you to consider that we have not discussed. The major point of this chapter is that the role of these different characteristics among substance-using persons is a major consideration that should not be ignored even though excessive drug use can affect people in similar ways. Overcoming an addiction necessarily must take into account these variations among persons. In the next chapter we discuss how you can determine whether or not the approach you are considering takes into account important differences.

CHAPTER 7

Selecting an Approach That Is Best for You

Before Getting Started

Throughout this book we have recommended that you become familiar with the treatment and self-help options currently available and then carefully consider your unique situation or the situation of the person in need of help to inform your decision about what to do. We have also encouraged you to think of your choices as being on a continuum from least intrusive to most intrusive, first seeking out the least intrusive course of action in resolving your addiction. In this chapter we provide you with information and suggestions about how to go about accomplishing that goal. Although natural recovery is among the possible choices that can be made (we discuss it in detail in Part Two), this chapter is concerned primarily with selecting treatment and self-help options.

Before starting we want to emphasize the importance of having familiarized yourself with the other material presented earlier in this book. While you may find the suggestions offered in this chapter helpful without exposure to that content, these recommendations will be of limited value if you have not read chapters 2 through 7. The strengths and weaknesses of treatment and self-help groups, the new approaches available, and your unique situation, among other considerations, are all relevant in selecting your best option. We urge you take full advantage of this information so that you can become an informed consumer of these services rather than simply "throwing the dice" and hoping for the best. Remember, the decision that you will make can hold profound, lifelong consequences.

This informed-consumer perspective assumes that you will not proceed with only limited information. If you are seeking assistance for another person, you are probably considering getting advice or have already obtained it from someone who is more informed about addiction treatment than you are. While this can be helpful, your friends, relatives, and neighbors who might provide this kind of information are generally unaware of the serious kinds of treatment and self-help issues discussed in chapters 2 through 7. They are unlikely to be familiar with the strengths and weaknesses of various forms of treatment, to know that a particular approach could be harmful to certain persons, to be aware of the newer treatment and self-help options, and they are unlikely to be informed about the host of concerns that surround treatment and self-help.

If you are seeking assistance for yourself, your situation is probably somewhat different. While the information that your friends, relatives, and neighbors might provide could also have the limitations discussed above, if you are the drug-dependent person chances are you already know something about the world of traditional treatment and 12-step groups. This is likely to be especially true if you use illicit street drugs and are a member of an informal network of drug users or of the street subculture. Chances are you know about one or more of the basic choices in your geographic area, and you might already have some familiarity with 12-step groups. If you are part of a heavy drinking subculture, you may also be somewhat familiar with what goes on in treatment and AA. Whether you or someone else has the drug problem and regardless of the limitations of your knowledge about treatment and self-help, few friends, relatives, and neighbors can provide you with the necessary in-depth understanding of these mainstay options to enable you to make truly informed decisions about using them.

Some people may also have access to someone who has undergone treatment or participated in self-help groups. Unquestionably, these persons have much to share with you about their experiences in treatment and/or self-help meetings, particularly as it pertains to activities within the particular program and/or meetings he or she has attended. Remember, however, that each person brings his or her own unique bias into those settings, thus people's experience with treatment and self-help meetings will be quite different. For example, if your source of information is someone who was highly motivated to stop using, he or she probably experienced treatment in a quite different way than someone resistant to change or even apathetic about it. Some people have only glowing comments about their treatment experience, while others may say, for example, that treatment was such a waste of time that they used drugs on the way home from the treatment facility. Those who have participated in 12-step groups may make the same kinds of comments. The point is that while those who have undergone treatment themselves and/or participated in self-help groups can provide you with useful information, such impressions come through the lenses of their own unique experience and should be viewed as such. We encourage you to visit some of these programs and/or attend open self-help meetings to get your own impressions firsthand.

Regardless of what additional information you are able to obtain from others, the options that are opened to you are determined by a number of factors. The three main factors are the urgency of your situation, the various treatment and self-help options available to you, and the resources that you have that can be drawn upon to take advantage of various treatment and self-help alternatives. Some individuals may be in great immediate danger because of their substance misuse, while others may simply be considering change because they are tired of the inconveniences and hassles they are experiencing. Most of the progressive treatments and newer self-help options are not available in every community, and limited financial resources will preclude using many of them. As we discuss how to go about finding the best intervention situation, we are mindful that your ability to examine various options may be more or less restricted by the above three factors. While we urge you not to rush too quickly into a treatment or self-help situation, we realize that you may not have the time to "shop around," nor the resources to be as selective as you might like to be.

In the next two sections of this chapter we provide illustrations and information that you can use to help you shop around for treatment and self-help groups that will likely meet your unique needs or the needs of someone you are assisting. We provide suggestions for locating these options and how to determine if, in fact, they are a good fit for you.

Choosing among Formal Treatment Options

As you begin to contemplate a course of treatment, take note of several key considerations about formal treatment. First, most formal treatment programs operate from similar theoretical and ideological frameworks. Most subscribe to the disease explanation of addiction and nearly all see abstinence as the primary treatment goal. However, it is important to note that some programs are less wedded to the disease theory of substance dependence and employ a range of techniques that draw on cognitive theory, behavioral theory, and other psychotherapeutic approaches to help their clients. Second, treatment can range from one or two one-hour educational sessions to permanent residence in a program for several years. These two extremes represent opposite ends of the treatment continuum from least intrusive to most intrusive, with many variations existing in between. Third, insurance companies and managed care organizations (MCOs) exercise substantial influence over the level and length of treatment, often not considering the individual treatment needs of the substance-dependent person. However, some private programs have developed creative arrangements with public-sector programs to provide additional care and aftercare for its clients when their treatment coverage has been exhausted.

How to Shop for a Good Fit

At the outset, shopping around for an appropriate addiction treatment facility might seem like an overwhelming task. How is one supposed to know about such programs and how to contact them? However, shopping for treatment is not unlike shopping for other products and services. Although there is no Consumer Reports available that rates the performance of various programs, with a little effort you can get information about nearly all treatment programs that exist in the United States, including specific information about those in your geographical area. One of easiest ways to find these programs is simply to look in the Yellow Pages of your local phone directory under "alcoholism" or "drug abuse." Most programs and many private practitioners who treat alcohol and other drug-dependent clients can be found in the Yellow Pages. Some of these phone listings also provide details about the types of services they offer. In some

Yellow Pages you will also find information about nationally known programs outside of your local area.

Another effective way to find treatment programs in your area is to go to the website for the Substance Abuse and Mental Health Services Administration (SAMHSA), www.samhsa.gov. SAMHSA offers a searchable directory of more than 11,000 treatment programs across the nation. Searches can be narrowed to specific cities and states and include maps identifying the location of each facility and basic information about each program. Perhaps the only drawback of using the SAMHSA directory is that many professional practitioners, such as psychologists and licensed clinical social workers, who work with substance abuse clients are not listed. Finally, all states have a state agency responsible for distributing funds and providing other assistance to alcohol and drug abuse treatment agencies throughout their state. These agencies, typically located in the state's capital, will have a statewide listing of most substance abuse treatment agencies.

Looking at a national directory such as the one developed by SAMHSA, will probably raise the question as to whether you want to seek the services of a local provider or one outside of your area. Although the remainder of this chapter should help you answer that question, a general rule of thumb is that persons who need highly specialized inpatient residential treatment, who would benefit more by leaving their environment than remaining in it, or who cannot find the services they need in their hometown area should consider services outside of their geographical areas by consulting the SAMHSA directory.

Information to Gather

Once you have a working list of program or service provider possibilities, you need to gather information from each of them to get a sense of the type of approach they take. While some of this information can be obtained by phone, we suggest that you actually visit the programs as you narrow your list down to serious considerations. The possibilities that you locate on the Internet, including some local treatment facilities, can be contacted through their websites, where they generally also provide a phone number.

What kind of information should you seek? Here is where chapter 6 becomes critically important in your search. Recall that there we talked about the unique personal and environmental situations in which substance-dependent persons live and how such factors necessarily influence how to go about making a decision. In that chapter we also made distinctions between the more popular kinds of drugs used and various implications of using them. Finally, we discussed several different use patterns and how they influence the severity of the problem. You should consider all of these factors as you begin to attempt to find a treatment fit for yourself or someone else. For your convenience, we briefly recap below the most significant implications of each of the factors discussed in chapter 6 or in other parts of the book.

Personal and Environmental Factors

Severity of Problem

▶ We recommend less intrusive types of treatment whenever possible, with the more long-term and intrusive types reserved for more severe cases.

▶ We recommend seeking independent assessments for severity of problem when possible, which should include more than merely the amount of use.

Level of Motivation

▶ Your level of motivation to change is the best predictor of success.

▶ If motivation to change is low, seek programs that are skilled at increasing the level of motivation through techniques such as motivational interviewing.

Gender

▶ The very unique needs of a substance-dependent woman must be considered in any treatment program.

▶ We recommend female-only treatment when possible and, at the very least, all-female group sessions in treatment.

Age

▶ Treatment for a young person should not mimic adult treatment.

▶ We discourage enrolling young persons in treatment that may label them a drug addict, alcoholic, or diseased.

Ethnicity

▶ Seek ethnically sensitive treatment where possible if you are a member of a minority group.

▶ Or, seek treatment that does not ignore or minimize the role of your ethnicity in your life.

Employment Status

▶ If you are employed and plan to enter treatment, consider how your employment will be affected by doing so, and be cautious with whom you share your plans.

▶ If you are unemployed, treatment planning should include securing satisfying employment for you as a priority goal; idle time after treatment can easily threaten all that you may achieve.

Education

▶ Those with higher levels of education can often benefit from less intrusive types of treatments such as outpatient counseling or introspective-oriented psychotherapy.

▶ Those with lower levels of education may need assistance beyond substance abuse treatment. If this is your situation, seek programs that emphasize and provide access to educational and vocational training opportunities.

Health Status

▶ Years of heavy substance dependency can create health problems that treatment programs must consider as part of treatment planning. Good treatment providers should be able to link you to needed health-care services.

▶ We highly recommend a thorough physical examination before you begin treatment.

Mental Health Status

▶ Since mental health difficulties may lead to or be the result of substance dependence, we recommend a thorough mental health assessment as soon as you are stabilized in treatment.

▶ A discernible amount of depression, restlessness, apathy, and other forms of mental discomfort can result when ending substance use. In most cases, these feelings pass with time; if they do not, mental health assistance may be required as part of treatment.

Resources

▶ If you have a substantial amount of resources, take advantage of them by being very selective about whom you entrust with your life.

▶ If your resources are few and your choices are limited to public-sector programs, still get as much information as you can so that you will find as good a fit as possible among them.

Social Environmental Factors

▶ If your drug use has caused you to become part of the street drug subculture and its related criminal activity, you will likely need more intrusive types of long-term treatment than someone who has been able to lead a more stable life and meet day-to-day responsibilities through conventional means.

▶ Treatment should not ignore the social environmental conditions in which your substance use occurred and your recovery expected. Being poor, a parent, a member of a faith-based organization, living in an impoverished neighborhood, and a range of other conditions should be considered for treatment to have a chance of succeeding.

Types of Drugs Used

Depressants

▶ If you are habituated to depressants such as alcohol, barbiturates, or tranquilizers, you might need medically supervised detoxification.

▶ Alcohol is the most widely abused drug in America, but because of its legal status it is a drug where moderation is an appropriate goal for some, generally for the less-problematic user.

Stimulants

▶ Treatment for stimulant dependence should address the similarities yet subtle differences between the range of effects that accompany use of cocaine, crack cocaine, methamphetamines, etc., as well as the related withdrawal effects of depression, lethargy, and other symptoms.

▶ If your stimulant use has caused you to become part of the street subculture, you will likely need more intrusive types of long-term treatment than someone who has maintained a conventional life.

Opiates

▶ While methadone maintenance has become an accepted form of treatment for addiction to opiates like heroin, we caution about enrolling in this form of treatment unless the dependence is extremely severe and has persisted for years.

▶ Long-term heroin use will invariably result in acquaintance with and participation in the street subculture, often accompanied by street crime. If you find yourself in this situation, more intrusive and long-term treatment is probably necessary.

Hallucinogens

▶ Hallucinogen use is generally associated with youth and does not create physical dependence, suggesting that most traditional forms of treatment are inappropriate.

▶ While hallucinogen use can be extremely dangerous, most young persons grow out of it. Private practitioners and others who specialize in working with these youth and their parents are in a better position to provide help than others.

Cannabis

▶ Marijuana use perplexes many treatment providers. While the consequences of use are often seen as rather benign, some persons clearly have problems with marijuana. If possible, seek treatment from someone in private practice who is skilled in working with marijuana users.

▶ Stay clear of programs that label marijuana users as drug addicts or as having a disease.

Inhalants

▶ Inhaling volatile chemicals is very dangerous and can result in irreversible brain damage. When inhalant use is suspected, seek help as quickly as possible from those skilled in working with inhalant users.

▶ For former inhalant users, we suggest a thorough mental and neurological examination along with close monitoring.

Club Drugs

▶ Because of the variety of club drugs available, your choice of help will depend on the type of drugs you used.

See chapter 6 and some of the above information regarding the various categories of drugs.

▶ Ecstasy is quickly becoming a national concern. The rise in its use precedes answers to questions about the dangers of use and what course of treatment is likely to be the most effective. Again, a skilled private practitioner might be the best place to begin when seeking help.

Use Patterns

How a Drug Is Taken

▶ If you are at the point of injecting drugs, a complete physical examination is suggested.

▶ Injecting heroin, cocaine, methamphetamines, and smoking crack cocaine might necessitate more intrusive and long-term treatment for you.

Extent of Use

▶ For those whose use is less chronic, less intrusive short-term types of treatment should be the first option, increasing intensity and duration only if success is not achieved.

▶ Chronic and long-term use might necessitate medically supervised detoxification. This can be particularly true for long-term users since they, like many substance abusers, often use more than one substance.

Level of Involvement in Drug Subculture

▶ As noted above, those who are overly immersed in the drug subculture and related street crime are likely to need more intrusive and extended treatment.

▶ Conversely, those with less involvement, who are able to straddle both the drug world and conventional life with its attendant responsibilities, will likely benefit from less intrusive, shorter-term treatments.

There are, of course, other factors one can consider in the above discussion, but we see these as the most critical. Your charge is to find a program that will respond to your unique situation or that of the person in need of help. In the following section, we provide six brief scenarios to further illustrate how such factors impact treatment choice. While none of these situations may apply exactly to the one you are concerned with, we think that knowing the distinctions between them will be helpful as you search for the best treatment fit for your particular situation.

Keisha

Keisha is a young, single, unemployed African American mother who has been on crack for four years. She receives Temporary Assistance for Needy Families (a new form of welfare) and has encountered difficulties with social services because of accusations from neighbors about neglect of her two children. For Keisha, a treatment choice might include, for example, an inpatient residential program that provides comprehensive services specifically designed to meet the multiple needs of poor minority women in such circumstances, ideally one with child-care services on site. Since Keisha is on federal assistance, her choices will probably be limited to public-sector programs or private programs that accept Medicaid or other forms of public funding to cover indigent care. Keisha's case manager will likely have enough information to give her some guidance in locating these programs.

Jay

Jay is a sixteen-year-old white male who smokes marijuana occasionally and pretty much keeps to himself at home. He does OK in school but probably not nearly as well as he could, given that he is a pretty bright adolescent. His parents have been horrified since they discovered his marijuana smoking and panicked about what to do. In Jay's case, one of the first concerns about a treatment program is that it should take into account the unique developmental needs of a young person, who should not be treated like an adult. Additionally, Jay's treatment should not label him a drug addict with a progressive incurable disease for the rest of his life, as marijuana use does not have the same reinforcing properties as drugs like alcohol, heroin, and tranquilizers. While marijuana use by a sixteen–year-old could be seen as a serious matter, or evolve into one, the problem may not be severe enough to warrant overly intrusive substance abuse treatment; such treatment might result in exposure to older persons with more serious problems, persons from the drug subculture who use heroin, cocaine, and other street drugs. A reasonable place to start is with basic harm reduction information or on family counseling, where the focus is not necessarily on substance abuse but on why Jay may feel alienated from his family.

Ellen

Ellen, 52, is a white, middle-class female homemaker who has successfully raised three children who have now gone on to start their own families. Ellen has sporadically taken medication without any major trouble to help her deal with the death of her husband and the stress of trying to raise three adolescents on her husband's pension and social security. However, since the children have all left, she began taking tranquilizers to excess and, unbeknownst to anyone else, she has developed a serious dependency on them, taking three to four times the recommended dosage. In considering a treatment approach that might respond to Ellen's situation, a plan should probably include medically supervised detoxification, since tranquilizers fall into the category of depressants. After detox, Ellen might respond to outpatient treatment with periodic follow-ups; however, her periodic episodes of taking psychotropic medication might indicate an underlying mental health problem that, if addressed, would also eliminate her need to use tranquilizers. As in many instances, inpatient residential care should be an option to consider only if other options have failed.

Antonio

Antonio, 32, is a Hispanic high school dropout who has on several occasions referred to himself as a "junkie." Most of his adult life has been spent as an intravenous heroin user with only sporadic interruptions when supplies were short or when he was incarcerated. Antonio deals drugs when he has access to a supplier and "hustles" on the streets to manage his addiction to heroin. He spent a couple of years enrolled in a public methadone maintenance program but was expelled from it when urine analyses determined that he continued to use other drugs in conjunction with the methadone. He has a lengthy criminal record and is facing several years in prison if convicted of his latest charge. His is a very serious situation. Antonio's long-term dependency on heroin, his extensive criminal history, and his many years on the streets suggest that he might be a candidate for long-term residential treatment. In addition to addressing his serious drug problem, he needs help functioning in the conventional world. He needs educational and vocational help along with a reorientation to and acceptance of conventional values. He is likely to need help with ordinary interpersonal and social skills that will help him effectively negotiate the normal world. In Antonio's case, one of the forms of treatment that could provide such extensive psychosocial services is a therapeutic community. Given his possible conviction on his impending charge, it is noteworthy that therapeutic communities are often used by the criminal justice system as an alternative to prison.

Patrick

Patrick, 55, is a white male plumber who has had problems off and on with alcohol for nearly twenty-five years. Because he now drinks nearly a fifth of vodka a day, his health is quickly failing and he is at risk of life-threatening illness if he continues to drink at this level. He is a devout churchgoer and family man but has simply let alcohol get the best of him. He has been successful at cutting back, but his drinking seems always to return to dangerously high levels. He has managed to retain his private health insurance for himself and his family. Of all the scenarios, Patrick's is probably the most ideal for traditional inpatient residential treatment. Clearly, he needs to abstain from drinking alcohol. The traditional Minnesota Model that will teach him about "the disease of alcoholism," whose treatment draws heavily on the principles of Alcoholics Anonymous (AA) and requires attending AA meetings, might resonate well with Patrick. His white male-identity, his alcohol-related illnesses, and his religious affinity are all factors that suggest he might be a good candidate for traditional, twenty-eight–day, inpatient residential treatment with aftercare. Given his daily use of large amounts of alcohol, medically supervised detoxification will be required prior to or in combination with treatment for alcohol dependency.

Dan

Dan, 34, is a successful African American male attorney who has been on a "cocaine run" for nearly four months. Dan drank alcohol socially, and occasionally he had used cocaine at parties for years without difficulty. But when he took a summer off from his busy practice to travel, he ended up snorting cocaine every day, throughout the entire summer. He also drank at night to help him fall asleep after using cocaine. Since he returned to work, he stopped using cocaine, but his drinking has increased to the point that it is interfering with work and family responsibilities. In Dan's case, even though his problem is of short duration, because the drug he is now using is alcohol, medically supervised detoxification might be called for and followed up with brief outpatient counseling. In fact, because alcohol use is legal and his problematic use has been rather short term, he might be a good candidate for moderation rather than abstinence and should probably seek the services of a provider who can help him accomplish that aim. Given Dan's advanced education and professional status, it may not be necessary for the provider to be as attuned to his ethnicity.

We do not expect the presentation of these six cases to make you an expert in appropriate treatment selection for persons with substance abuse problems. However, we hope that the differences among them demonstrate that appropriate treatment for a person's problem must respond to the uniqueness of his or her situation. These scenarios also underscore the

importance of shopping around for an approach that responds to such important individual differences.

Cautions

The discussion of the above cases illustrates an important
practical lesson to keep in mind as you gather information
from the various programs you are considering. If a program
representative says something to the effect that "addiction is
addiction," implying that the various factors of age, gender,
environmental conditions, severity of use, and so on do not
matter, you should proceed with caution or look elsewhere.

You need to be aware of several other cautions related to
selecting treatment programs. First, through comprehensive
assessment techniques, many credible programs have the
ability to determine the necessary level of intervention appropriate for different types of clients. Such assessments attempt to determine whether a person might benefit from a
particular form of inpatient residential treatment or from a
less intrusive variation of outpatient services. And, where
programs have an array of different kinds of attractive public-sector services to offer, one's options for the appropriate
level of treatment can be quite good. Conversely, comprehensive assessment interviews can reveal a need for certain
kinds of services that simply are not available in a particular
community; examples are moderation training and inpatient
residential programs that offer a non-disease approach to
treatment. Furthermore, many programs gather extensive

information from their clients but then do not take full advantage of that information to guide decisions about what kind of treatment or referral to offer. Still other programs claim to match treatment with the particular situation of the service seeker, but are in fact one-size-fits-all programs, where most clients are run through similar, if not identical, treatment activities. Because in many communities treatment options are severely limited, some people will need to be creative in finding a good fit for themselves or their loved ones. Placing a person in an inappropriate treatment program will likely not lead to the kind of results you want and, in some cases, can actually be harmful.

Staff

While most treatment programs tend to subscribe to the disease view of addiction, the approach of staff in a treatment facility can be the determining factor between a good or poor program. Many staff are able to integrate other theoretical principles into their approach to treatment and make real differences with clients, even those who find disease-based principles questionable. Although many programs rely heavily on recovering persons to staff their facilities, research suggests that whether one has personally had a drug problem or not is irrelevant to one's effectiveness as a substance abuse counselor. And, while there are many competent recovering counselors in these programs, many others are less effective. Some are simply under-trained in areas of human behavior, human motivation, human diversity, and the like. Others rely too much on approaches that helped them personally to the exclusion of newer, more promising possibilities. Many of these staff work in facilities where they once received services and are deeply wedded to these programs' philosophies. Some continue to attend 12-step meetings and are intolerant of other self-help approaches.

We believe that those who have overcome addictions deserve an opportunity to use their personal insights to help others if they choose to do so. We also believe that with the appropriate level of training (beyond that generally required for addiction counselor certification), they have much to offer those struggling with substance dependence. However, if they themselves have not yet completely resolved their own drug problem, there is reason for concern. If their conceptualization of effective treatment is very limited or they are unaware of the more complex biopsychosocial issues that create and sustain substance dependency, their ability to be effective treatment providers could be limited.

We tend to be a bit more optimistic about programs whose therapeutic staff consists primarily of persons with advanced professional training. Programs that employ primarily recovering counselors tend to be a bit inflexible, and they do not fully appreciate much of the new research that challenges old ideas. Moreover, programs where the top administrator is vocal about being in recovery and is attending 12-step meetings give us considerable pause. Also know that because a person is a psychologist, clinical social worker, or other mental health professional does not preclude his or her past drug use. In our training of master's and doctoral students, we have encountered many students who have overcome substance dependence, both with and without treatment. As with persons in recovery, some are drawn to the field because of their own personal experiences. However, they tend to be discrete about sharing their past and generally do not refer to themselves as "in recovery."

It is also important to note in this discussion about staff that no amount of training will compensate for poor interpersonal and communication skills when working with clients. The first step of effective counseling and psychotherapy is to create a climate of trust that results in a genuine working relationship with the person seeking help. While we tend to favor counselors with professional training over those with only personal experience, one still needs to "connect" with the client or little else is even possible.

Find out about the composition of the program's staff at the various facilities you are considering. Because a professional staff costs the agencies much more financially, the level of this financial commitment can be a reflection of the organization's commitment to quality treatment.

Getting Information from Staff

You can get a lot of information about various programs and the services they offer by simply calling these facilities on the phone. Most also have pamphlets, booklets, or other printed materials about their program that they will mail to you if you request them. This can be a good way to begin your inquiry. However, as your search begins to narrow, we suggest that you actually visit the programs you are considering. During your visit, ask the questions that may have come up after you had familiarized yourself with their printed materials. Because of varying confidentiality standards among treatment programs, you may or may not see actual clients during your visit. Below we offer ten examples of the kinds of questions whose answers can be very revealing to prospective clients. We will show how the responses to them can be instructive for you. The answers to some of these questions may be found in the program's printed materials, or they may not apply to a particular facility you are visiting.

(1) How similar is your program to the Minnesota Model? Programs that rely heavily on the Minnesota Model to guide their treatment activities represent the traditional treatment programs discussed in chapters 2 and 3. By definition, such programs are guided by the disease explanation of substance dependence and rely heavily on 12-step group principles and activities. If you have determined that this form of treatment is what you need, the answer to this question will let you know if you have located one. However, if you need something different, you will likely want to seek a program that does not subscribe to this approach.

(2) What are the credentials of your professional staff? Recall our discussion above about over-reliance on staff in recovery and how resources spent on staff can be very telling. Quality programs may have persons in recovery on their staffs, but, in our view, the bulk of the staff should be

professionally trained, with graduate degrees. Additionally, most professional persons, as part of their professional education, are generally trained in one or more forms of counseling or psychotherapy and tend to be more open to alternative approaches. Persons who have this kind of training hold a distinct advantage over those who have not or those exposed only to drug counselor certification training. The professional will likely be certified as a drug counselor but also be licensed to practice psychotherapy; the person in recovery will most likely be certified only as a drug counselor.

(3) How strictly does your program adhere to the disease explanation of addiction? Some substance-dependent persons find the disease explanation of addiction very appealing and even relieving. For others, however, overemphasis on the disease view can be a major turnoff. Some staff within disease-based programs are, however, also very skilled in various forms of counseling and psychotherapy that depart sharply from the principles of the disease theory. Such persons are able to engage and assist clients in spite of the clients' discomfort with some aspects of the overall program.

(4) Given the characteristics of the person seeking help, how will the program respond specifically to his or her unique needs? We have tried to emphasize here the importance of treatment that responds to the unique situation of the addicted person. One-size-fits-all treatment is inappropriate and ineffective. If the person seeking help is a female, for example, we recommend programs designed for females. For

coed programs, we recommend female-only groups, female counselors for females, and the like.

(5) Does your program provide case management services? Many persons, particularly those with limited resources, need case management services in addition to their participation in counseling, groups, and other drug abuse treatment activities. Case management identifies and connects persons with critically needed resources that both aid the process of giving up drugs and help meet basic needs necessary to a smooth transition into a productive life. For example, when lack of employment skills is a barrier for a person, case management services may attempt to locate and connect that person with appropriate vocational-training opportunities. These kinds of activities can be carried out by counselors or a case manager hired specifically for such purposes.

(6) What types of clients do you currently serve? People can be very uncomfortable and even frightened when confronted with interacting and living among others with whom they do not share values, cultures, and beliefs. While in some ways such situations hold the potential of being enriching, they can also pose problems. Make sure that the composition of the clients in a program does not present a major barrier for the person enrolling in it.

(7) What is your program's position on clients attending 12-step groups, and is your staff familiar with a number of other types of new groups that depart from 12-step philosophy?

Of course, in many areas 12-step groups are the only self-help groups available, and the staff may not have other options. However, groups like Women for Sobriety and Rational Recovery have been around long enough that the staff should at least be familiar with them, even if they are not available in their particular area. In most large urban areas, these newer groups are available and should be part of a menu of options for clients. It is also important to know whether or not a program requires attendance at a 12-step meeting. Self-help group participation should never be a requirement for successful recovery, only an option.

(8) Does your program use principles of motivational interviewing? This is a technique that is gaining popularity among more sophisticated programs. It is a technique that essentially dismisses the widely held notion that you must "break through the denial," "break them down so you can build them up," and other outdated confrontational techniques that have not been proven by research to be superior to other clinically accepted interviewing techniques. With motivational interviewing, ambivalence or resistance to change is seen as a natural reaction to the threat of loss of freedom of choice. Rather than the counselor imposing his or her views about the necessity to change, the client is engaged in a way that the choice and gradual commitment to change comes from him or her. In our view, programs that employ motivational interviewing techniques have an edge over programs that employ more authoritarian techniques.

(9) What is your program's position on abstinence versus reduced use of the legal drug alcohol? While most programs continue to see abstinence as the only goal for its clients, more and more research suggests that reduced use of alcohol might be a more reasonable goal for certain types of alcohol-using clients. Programs where staff are not so wedded to the necessity of abstinence for all its alcohol-using clients and have activities in place that reflect that position are more likely to be progressive and to highly value individuality as well as self-determination. Such programs are likely to have in place abstinence promoting activities when reduction efforts are not successful.

(10) How do you manage situations where clients in your program are still in need of treatment but are at the limits of their insurance or MCO coverage? Although funders of public-sector programs also set limits on funding for client care, this question is more likely to be instructive when exploring for-profit programs. The response to this question might give you a real sense for the level of commitment that a program has to its clients when there is no financial incentive to do so.

There are any number of questions that you can ask program staff that will help you determine whether or not a particular facility is a good fit for you or the person in need of assistance. While some of these above might be relevant in your search, we encourage you to come up with questions that relate to your unique situation so you can obtain the best information for yourself.

Self-Help Groups

When shopping around for an appropriate self-help group to fit your particular situation, there are a few things to remember. The most important is that, although in this chapter we are separating treatment from self-help groups, attending these groups can actually be seen as a form of treatment. Clients may attend these meetings in conjunction with other types of treatment or as part of aftercare once treatment is completed.

As in the case of treatment, some self-help groups are more intrusive than others. Some suggest that their participants attend meetings for the remainder of their lives. Other groups discourage long-term attendance, warning persons of the dangers of over-reliance on meetings to the detriment of self-sufficiency. In fact, as discussed in chapter 5, Rational Recovery (RR) discourages attending ongoing meetings. Instead, RR recommends that its participants acquire training on addictive voice recognition. RR might be seen as the least intrusive of all of these self-help groups. The philosophy that addiction is a lifelong disease that requires lifelong vigilance by attending meetings places 12-step groups at the other end of the continuum. Another important point here is that 12-step groups are the most readily available of all self-help groups across the United States. One can find AA meetings in almost any community in the nation. Other 12-step groups such as Narcotics Anonymous and Cocaine Anonymous are also very accessible in some communities. If, however, you are interested in groups such as Women for Sobriety, SMART, or others of the newer groups discussed in chapter 5, your chance of having access to them is much lower. While most of these groups are growing, lack of access to them is a major barrier for improvement for those who would attend support group meetings but do not find 12-step meetings appealing.

Another important consideration is that if you want to access these newer groups, your best source will be the Internet. In many areas there is no listing of them in the phone book or anyplace else. However, you can go to their websites and find a list of meetings; many, of course, are in large urban areas. All of these websites also provide information about how to start groups, and many persons wanting access to alternative self-help groups actually take on that task. As we noted in chapter 5, individuals can also attend meetings online in chatrooms.

If you are leaning toward attending self-help meetings, we suggest you attend meetings in different locations. In the case of AA meetings, this can be a relatively easy process since many such open meetings are offered in most areas. In fact, as previously mentioned, in certain communities you can find AA meetings created to meet the specific needs of different groups; for example, women, professionals, and non-smokers. Opportunities to attend a variety of other meetings, even 12-step meetings like NA and CA, are generally not as great. And, as suggested above, in the case of the newer self-help groups options can be quite limited or even nonexistent.

Conclusion

Whether you choose treatment or self-help options, it is critically important that you understand what you are getting yourself or someone else into. We hope that reading the chapters in this part of the book will put you in a better position to do that. We encourage you to look at the websites we have identified, as well as others you might find. Get acquainted with what is out there and on the horizon of substance abuse treatment and self-help. Familiarize yourself with various controversies, debates, and opposing views about the current state of treatment and self-help groups. Think of it this way: if you decide on treatment, you are about to purchase services that range anywhere in cost from $100 to $60,000, with the average cost of inpatient residential treatment at $1,000 per day in some areas. And, although you may or may not be paying for this service out of your own pocket, someone will be paying lots of money for your care. Given this, you have not only a right to know exactly what you are purchasing, you have an obligation to do so.

◀ PART TWO ▶

QUITTING
ON YOUR
OWN

CHAPTER 8

Quitting the Natural Way:
Is Natural Resolution for You?

In an earlier chapter we discussed some of the major strengths and weaknesses of enrolling in traditional treatment. With natural recovery, or quitting on your own, many of these weaknesses associated with treatment are mitigated or do not present the same level of risk. There are, in fact, several major advantages to this course of resolution when compared to undergoing formal treatment or joining self-help groups. The first section of this chapter introduces several of those key advantages of natural recovery over the alternatives.

Before identifying them, it is critically important that we point out that this path may not be a realistic option for all who suffer from alcohol and other drug addictions. While research on natural recovery suggests that most people overcome substance abuse problems on their own, the experiences of those in our studies and the studies of others suggest that successful self-recovery is contingent upon certain conditions that should be carefully considered. As you will see later in this chapter, there are specific personal and social factors that increase the probability of successful self-recovery as well as factors that make such a choice an ill-advised one.

With that said, the major advantages of natural recovery advantages include: less addict identity and stigma, an increased sense of self-efficacy, an increased sense of individual empowerment, less life disruption, and a smaller financial burden. For a more detailed discussion of these advantages, anchored in the related theoretical and empirical literature, see our other book, *Coming Clean: Overcoming Addiction without Treatment.*

Reduced Addict Identity and Stigma

Enrolling in treatment or joining traditional self-help groups is a significant departure from conventional life and related day-to-day activities and can cause a significant interruption of the normal identity-formation processes. The consequences of this identity interruption, or shift in identity, can be dramatic. For many users, the act of entering treatment serves as a symbolic declaration that he or she is, indeed, an alcoholic and/or a drug addict. Moreover, most treatment programs that one is likely to enter currently subscribe to the belief (though it is an unsubstantiated one) that addiction is a progressive and lifelong disease, an idea that can hold substantial identity-related consequences. The act of entering treatment opens the door to being reacted to by others as an alcoholic and/or drug addict, and, consequently, to seeing oneself as such. Although people today have generally become more accepting of persons with substance abuse problems, being thought of as an alcoholic or drug addict unfortunately continues to carry substantial social stigma. These negative images in the minds of others can create subtle and not-so-subtle barriers for the former user, including negative gossip, stereotyping, exclusion, ostracism, and, in some cases, outright cruelty.

A different level of concern is that formal treatment requires the maintenance of a formal record of a person's participation in that treatment. While there are currently laws in place to protect the confidentiality of such records, documenting treatment participation can be potentially detrimental and, in some cases, may actually compound an already difficult situation. For example, various applications for employment, licenses, certifications, and health, life, and mortgage insurance often include questions about one's participation in alcohol and drug treatment programs. To think that answering in the affirmative on these application forms is inconsequential is simply naïve. One should consider that the Medical Information Bureau has access to treatment participation documentation, as discussed in chapter 3, and in many instances one's involvement in treatment can be detected. Also, with increasing storage of such records on computer files, computer hackers have access to information about people's private lives. Note also that some professionals occasionally share information with their families and friends about their clients or patients.

Participating in self-help groups represents a somewhat different kind of challenge to one's anonymity. As a rite of passage, a person seeking help is required to proclaim, in the presence of a roomful of total strangers, that she or he is an alcoholic and/or drug addict. While members of these groups promulgate the principle of anonymity, new recruits are still encouraged to admit their alcohol and drug-related wrongdoings to others outside the group as well. Although such action might, at times, be therapeutically beneficial, it can simultaneously subvert anonymity by calling attention to one's circumstance. There is generally no formal record of one's participation in self-help groups and anonymity is observed as an intrinsic principle, but there is some risk of exposing one's past transgressions. More importantly, the lifelong label of alcoholic and/or drug addict inherent in traditional self-help programs could be a price too high to pay for some.

Increased Sense of Self-Efficacy

Another advantage to self-recovery is the increased sense of self-efficacy that can be associated with solving a substance abuse problem without professional assistance. Self-efficacy is a term used by social psychologists for the idea that as persons gradually become more and more proficient in overcoming obstacles in a particular area of their lives, they simultaneously begin to feel more confident in their abilities to overcome obstacles in other areas of their lives as well. Their overall confidence and related optimism about their ability to successfully negotiate life in general increases or is reaffirmed. Albert Bandura, one of the leading social psychologists who has studied self-efficacy, feels that the belief in one's self-efficacy is critical in aiding or hindering individual's as they go about their daily activities:

> [People] who have a high sense of efficacy visualize success scenarios that provide positive guides for performance. Those who judge themselves as inefficacious are more inclined to visualize failure scenarios that undermine performance by dwelling on how things will go wrong.

For Bandura, the traits associated with someone who is self-efficacious include a sense of self-determination, motivation, goal attainment, and confidence. Self-efficacy increases an individual's resiliency as well as capacity to function in effective ways and under a variety of conditions. The self-remitters we studied lead us to believe that when persons overcome severe and long-standing drug problems on their own, their self-efficacy is enhanced.

Individual Empowerment

The concept of empowerment is very similar to self-efficacy. The term has gained considerable acceptance over the last two decades in professional helping circles and is now increasingly used in public discourse. Both empowerment and self-efficacy denote an increased sense of mastery over life's obstacles by making choices and executing strategies that result in one's increased capacity to solve immediate as well as future problems. The principle difference between the terms is that empowerment generally refers to groups and communities; it also tends to highlight strengths and competencies, natural helping systems, and proactive behaviors within the environment in which people exist. The term "empowerment" compels us to think of wellness versus illness, competence versus deficits, and strengths versus weaknesses. When people cultivate their potential strengths, draw upon existing natural networks, and cultivate community resources to solve pressing personal problems, they are personifying the concept of empowerment. Those who study empowerment observe that the methods used to solve one's problems can be as important in creating a sense of power as the act of solving the problem.

The strategies used by those in our studies and the results of their efforts to arrest their alcohol and drug problems without entering treatment personify empowerment. These strategies included drawing upon inner strengths, finding support within the naturally existing relationships of family and friends, and avoiding toxic relationships and traditional treatment institutions. Thus, from this perspective, a major advantage of self-recovery is that it can foster individual empowerment.

Less Disruption

While disruption of addiction and the activities that support it are clearly the goals of resolution both with and without treatment, disruption of other conventional life activities due to long-term treatment can be extremely problematic for some. Undergoing treatment, including attending group meetings, can be very disruptive. These disruptions assume different levels of importance depending on the unique situation of the individual seeking help and the course of treatment he or she pursues. For example, women who serve as the primary caregivers for young children might find these disruptions overwhelming if, as is often the case, treatment isolates them from their children, thus preventing them from meeting their parental responsibilities. For single mothers who may be at risk for temporary and, in extreme cases, permanent loss of their children if they begin a course of formal treatment, the implications can be profound. For the individual who is the primary income earner in a family, particularly if that person is employed in the secondary labor market that offers little job flexibility or leave opportunities, enrolling in treatment, even briefly, can result in loss of income and even loss of a job.

Long-term residential treatment such as therapeutic communities can require a commitment to treatment of one to three years. While most agree that participation in self-help groups is generally less disruptive than undergoing most formal treatment, others maintain that 12-step group involvement can actually be quite disruptive. They observe that participation in these groups can result in more, rather than less, disruption since new members are encouraged to attend meetings daily, particularly during the first ninety days of their participation. There is also the potential for significant disruption due to the principle of lifelong participation espoused and practiced by some of these groups' members.

Natural resolution is at the opposite end of this spectrum. People are not required to become residents of hospitals, treatment centers, or other institutions for extended periods of time and are not encouraged to attend inordinate numbers or a lifetime of meetings. This is not to suggest that self-recovery is completely free of disruptions and logistical challenges. Natural resolvers have reported making fundamental and difficult changes in their lives in order to arrest their addictions. However, the disruptions associated with recovery without treatment are more natural than artificial, and are consistent with other growth-promoting change strategies that non-drug dependent persons employ throughout their lives. They are inherently self-imposed strategies that are flexible enough to allow individuals to maintain and expand upon their conventional roles and responsibilities. The logistics of rearranging one's life to enter an inpatient residential treatment facility, particularly for extended periods, can be monumental.

Reduced Financial Burden

The absence of the financial burden associated with treatment is an obvious advantage of natural recovery that can be easily appreciated. While the financial burdens associated with self-help groups are negligible, formal addiction treatment can be extremely costly and, for many, prohibitive. Whether the treatment facility is a private agency, a public agency, or some combination of both, treatment is expensive. The cost of treatment in the twenty-eight–day inpatient residential program at the Betty Ford Clinic in California was $14,700 at the time of this writing, and $15,900 at the popular Hazelden Foundation program in Minnesota. Local inpatient residential treatment in the Denver area, on the average, cost approximately one thousand dollars per day. On the other hand, the financial burden for those who self-resolve is minimal. For many, much of the actual cost of such treatment is actually incurred by insurance companies and managed care organizations, but others pay for these services themselves.

Who Is a Good Candidate for Recovery without Treatment?

At this point, you might wonder if you feel that you would be better off trying to solve your problem on your own. You may have already reached the conclusion that formal treatment or participation in self-help groups is not for you at this particular moment. Although you have been introduced to a number of nontraditional substance abuse treatment techniques and treatment approaches as well as new types of self-help groups, you might still feel that formal assistance of any kind is something that you would rather avoid, at least at this time. On the other hand, you may have purchased this book simply because you are primarily interested in the content of Part Two: you or someone you care about could be struggling with substance dependency, and you want to know how people can stop without enrolling in an alcohol and drug treatment program or without attending self-help groups.

In either case, we applaud your decision; we think that of all of the types of change strategy options, self-recovery is ideal for many. Much of our own research and academic writing has been in the area of natural recovery from addiction, and we think that the advantages to this path of quitting that we discussed in the first section of this chapter are quite compelling. Our many years of research and writing about this subject also suggest to us that there are certain situations under which self-recovery will have a greater probability of succeeding than other methods. In the second section of this chapter we identify these conditions that are likely to foster a successful self-recovery effort. In a sense, we actually provide you with a general profile of the type of person for whom self-recovery is likely to have a reasonable chance of succeeding.

Characteristics and Conditions

As we discussed earlier, personal attributes as well as the environmental conditions in which a person uses, abuses, and becomes dependent on intoxicating or otherwise mind-altering substances can play a major role in one's ability to successfully overcome addiction. Characteristics such as level of education, vocational and professional skills, pro-social values, and mental health status represent a few of the personal attributes that should be considered when one is attempting cessation-with or without treatment. Similarly, environmental conditions such as socioeconomic background of family, community membership, subculture membership, and network of relationships are a few examples of such environmental conditions.

Those who have been able to successfully overcome severe alcohol and drug problems without entering treatment or participating in self-help groups, appear to have in common certain personal qualities and live in similar day-to-day environmental conditions that increase the probability of success. These characteristics and conditions often intersect in ways that make them somewhat difficult to separate. We will not attempt to do so here but rather present ten characteristics of such persons:

1. They tend to be high school graduates, many with college or more advanced degrees.
2. Most have vocational or professional skills, or otherwise are employable and are generally employed during their addictions. Of these, many are self-employed.
3. Overall, they tend to have the verbal skills that allow them to verbally express themselves and interact in various social settings.

4. They are often introspective, with an ability to self-evaluate their behavior and make appropriate plans and choices to solve problems.

5. During their substance dependency periods, many continue to have access to friends and meaningful relationships with others who do not have substance abuse problems.

6. The mental health of nearly all the people we interviewed in our studies was good. Among the few who had experienced mental health problems, such problems were not severe.

7. Most hold conventional pro-social values such as family life, the desire to be successful, the importance of a career, and a concern for how others perceive them.

8. Those who used illicit drugs like heroin and cocaine appear to be able to successfully straddle both the illicit drug subculture and the culture of conventional life.

9. Among those who have had contact with the criminal justice system, such contact tends to be in the form of DUI offenses or minimal legal infractions and incarcerations. They generally cannot be characterized as hard-core criminals.

10. Overall, through their recovery, they came to see themselves as part of a family and a community.

It is evident that the types of people who are able to solve their addiction on their own are not overly immersed in the drug world. Their drug problem is the major distinguishing characteristic that separates them from others who live conventional lives. In another sense, however, they are somewhat different from a large group of substance-dependent persons whose social stability has been compromised, who have alienated themselves from family, who are unemployable, and who have been in and out of prison for drug-related offenses and criminal activity. From the list above, it is easy to see how simple it would be to identify these characteristics and conditions that may also impair a self-recovery effort.

This list should not be seen as an exhaustive index of all of the characteristics and conditions of persons who are likely to succeed at self-recovery. We present it simply for the sake of illustration and include core qualities that we, along with other researchers, have discovered to be especially relevant to a successful natural recovery. There are no doubt innumerable other situations we have not listed above that could also have substantial influences on the probability of success. Of course, these qualities do not necessarily assure one of successful recovery. Just as there are many cases of affluent people who have struggled with addiction for years with little success, there are also success stories among those mired in poverty in inner-city neighborhoods where alcohol and drug use is rampant. Those who do not possess the listed qualities should not assume that self-recovery is impossible for them; it may simply be more challenging.

We conclude by reminding the reader that we have found that very few behaviors that are part of our human experience are invulnerable to the power of human resolve.

CHAPTER 9

Initial Challenges to Self-Change

In this and the next two chapters we identify key strategies that have been used successfully by persons who have overcome addictions unaided by treatment or 12-step groups. The material in this chapter is presented in the spirit of offering what we consider key practical suggestions and is not intended to represent the entire range of strategies that individuals have actually employed.

Starting Out on Natural Recovery

Before you embark upon a "natural" road to recovery, it is important first to address several key issues that you will need to consider as you contemplate self-recovery. While each person's situation is unique, there are five questions that every person needs to ask himself or herself before pursuing natural recovery. These questions include: Do I have the desire to change? What is my personal plan for change? Do I have the resources to implement my plan? Should I share my plans with others? And, do I need to adopt a regime of complete abstinence?

Do I Have the Desire to Change?

One of the fundamental observations of many involved in psychology, social work, counseling, and other helping professions is that people's resistance to change or their uncertainty about the need to change is a major obstacle to personal improvement. In fact, among professionals who treat alcohol and drug dependent persons, motivation to eliminate intake of alcohol and/or drugs is seen as a necessary condition for this change actually to occur. Within many treatment programs, providing opportunities for clients to create a strong desire to change is an integral part of program planning and structure.

This same principle applies to self-recovery; that is, even the most elegant plans for recovery are likely to render disappointing results without a sincere desire on the part of the substance dependent person to change. Like the self-remitters we interviewed in our studies on natural recovery, you must have a reason to initiate a change in your life.

A reasonable place to begin would be to ask yourself, "Why should I quit?" Alcohol and drug dependent persons have a hard time quitting when they perceive that they are benefiting from continued use. Even in the midst of assorted personal and interpersonal problems, people can still derive pleasure and profound meaning from using mind-altering substances. While the significance of such benefits is often not readily apparent or understandable to those unfamiliar with substance dependence, such benefits are no less real. For example, people from disadvantaged circumstances with limited education, few employment opportunities, diminished faith in conventional values, feeling a sense of hopelessness in their lives, might decide they have little reason to quit. Their feelings of alienation, coupled with many opportunities to use both alcohol and illicit drugs and their status within the drug subculture, can hold strong appeal. Similarly, continued use of alcohol and drugs to ward off discomfort created by compromised mental health could be seen as very rational. While in the long run chronic use of these substances can compound mental health difficulties and other stressful conditions, the immediate, albeit temporary, relief that use provides can be a compelling reason for some to continue their habit.

For many, the benefits of avoiding the discomfort of temporary, and in some cases protracted, withdrawal symptoms can be a major motivational barrier. The essential point is that in order to overcome addiction, you must first develop a strong desire to change your life, one that counters the perceived benefits of continued use. Starting out on natural recovery from this position will substantially increase your chances for success. Interestingly, and perhaps understandably, many people who successfully quit report that their reason to change was actually solidified during a using state. Although this decision was often gradual, one that continued to form as conditions in their lives worsened, the final commitment to act was made while "under the influence." Clearly, we would not encourage you to put yourself at further risk by using drugs to arrive at a decision to commit yourself to quit, but we do think that it is important for you to know that many people actually finalize their resolve to stop while in this state. Such a conclusion might easily be dismissed as a fleeting thought while "high," but if these thoughts occur frequently to a person, he or she could be entering the initial phase of change.

Moreover, many researchers have identified "ambivalence about quitting" and/or "lack of motivation to quit" as part of the normal process of recovery. We agree, but we would add that ambivalence and motivation are not impenetrable static states immune to manipulation by the person experiencing these feelings. Many skilled counselors have developed techniques that acknowledge these states but also employ creative strategies to decrease the ambivalence and increase the motivation. A technique for increasing motivation and reducing ambivalence is to perform a simple, but sincere, cost-benefit analysis on your substance-using behavior. List all of the benefits that accrue to you by using. Then list what the personal cost is-financially, psychologically, socially, and physically. Do the same for quitting. Ask yourself about the benefits and personal costs of stopping your use of alcohol and other drugs. While the simplicity of this exercise is obvious, it can be surprisingly powerful for some. Those who actually list these costs and benefits on paper often become hard-pressed to ignore the irrationality of their continued destructive substance use.

Also, it is important to remember that reducing ambivalence and increasing motivation are not one-point-in-time events; both are best understood as a process, often a gradual one. While we know of many cases where people were successful on their very first attempts, frequently they begin the journey of recovery and fail; and sometimes they only last a few days or weeks. Do not become discouraged; this is not unusual. If you are reasonably sincere, your ability to remain on course increases with time.

Finally, we think it is critical during this early period that the user does not buy into the old adage of "once an addict, always an addict." Besides being wrong, such popular myths can have demoralizing effects on the motivation of the person undertaking this change. As persons wane back and forth between using and not-using periods, it is important they realize that while change can be difficult and progress gradual, the pharmacological properties of drugs are no match for the resolve of the human spirit.

What Is My Personal Plan for Change?

As in the case of other major life changes, ending substance dependence is an undertaking that is best approached thoughtfully and strategically. We encourage you to adopt a proactive rather than reactive posture that anticipates obstacles and challenges along the way. Having a plan for this change, even if only a rough one, will go far in increasing your chances for success. While this kind of change can result in feelings of frustration, discomfort, and overall uneasiness, thoughtful planning can minimize negative experiences that might diminish chances for success.

As part of your planning process, you should avoid "just letting things happen." This can result in the return to old ways and habits. There are a variety of questions you could begin to consider: When should I begin the process of self-recovery? Will I gradually reduce my substance use over a period of time, or will I stop abruptly? Will I need to take time away from work? Will it be necessary to remove myself from the surrounding environment by temporarily, or even permanently, relocating? What personal strengths and resources can I most rely on for change? Where are my primary social support groups that can help me reach my goals? How will my effort affect my family or those who are close to me? Thoughtful planning can help you think about these questions as well as other questions you will need to ask yourself and simultaneously help you begin to identify appropriate action. Later, when we discuss actual recovery strategies, the relevancy of planning to successful recovery will become even more apparent.

Though planning can be a crucial component of the process of natural recovery, it is also important to caution against overplanning. While structure and a sense of predictability can be critical in the early phase, too many plans can put inordinate amounts of pressure on you; perhaps even setting you up to fail. This problem can be further compounded when these expectations are not met, resulting in frustration, doubts about your ability to succeed, and lowered confidence. Furthermore, you should be somewhat flexible in your planning since you can never fully anticipate the array of life circumstances likely to be encountered as you move forward in this change process.

Should I Share Plans with Others?

Because of the profound negative effects that drug and alcohol addiction can have on family members and others who are close to you, sharing with them specific plans to change can be interpreted as making a commitment to them. Sharing these intentions with them may also help you identify a network of family members, friends, coworkers, and other associates who can be used as support systems. While such natural support systems can be extremely valuable, our work in the area of natural recovery suggests that the person attempting to make the change should be careful about whom they share their plans with. Expectations held by others can have both positive and negative effects on your effort. On the one hand, sharing your intentions can produce a sense of accountability to others, create support networks, and generate strong motivation to succeed. On the other, however, these same expectations, particularly in the early stages of a recovery effort, might lead others to make unreasonable demands on you that may put you at risk for using again. Unfortunately, because the belief in the necessity of treatment is so widely pervasive in our society, some well-meaning people might not accept as sincere your claims about doing it on your own. They may instead prescribe an abrupt "straight and narrow" course of recovery that precludes the kind of gradual and often wavering process that many persons experience before they finally overcome substance dependence.

Sharing one's plans with others can also compound feelings of failure and inadequacy when success is not immediately achieved. These feelings could reinforce widely held myths about addiction and suggest that self-recovery is, in fact, impossible. Popular beliefs held by others such as "once an addict, always an addict" or other diseased-based myths can create major obstacles to natural recovery and hold important implications in your attempt to change. Conversely, by undertaking natural recovery independent of the traditional expectations and beliefs of others, you might be able to minimize unfortunate setbacks by reframing them, not as failure but as a necessary progression toward eventual change. Change takes time, and you may not be successful the first time around.

While we do not want to discourage you from taking full advantage of existing relationships that can aid your effort, given the prevailing myths about substance dependency- myths that run counter to volumes of research, we simply wish to alert you to the pros and cons of sharing your plans with others. In ideal cases, it will mean sharing plans and gaining support from those who accept and validate your desire to change in your own way and at your own pace. These are the people that will help bolster your confidence, unlike those who would constantly remind you of your "disease."

The latter group can have toxic and corrosive effects on the sincerest of recovery plans.

Do I Need to Practice Abstinence?

The decision to pursue a course of abstinence versus having as your goal the reduction of substance use is an important consideration and a decision that many contemplating this kind of change struggle with. This is a very touchy subject for some in the treatment field. Even in the face of scientific evidence that many people reduce their substance use to less destructive levels, much of their orientation suggests that abstinence is the only reasonable goal. While many might believe this to be the most appropriate course of action, it is erroneous to assume that the only path to success is abstinence. Many people, even after many years of chronic alcohol or drug dependence, are able to reduce harmful intake of these substances without completely terminating use altogether. Many others who have used for years and have had problems might be characterized only as problem users or substance abusers rather than substance dependents. Nevertheless, though reduction of use might be an appropriate goal for some, for others such a goal after varied failed attempts to reduce use would be unreasonable.

Among these self-remitters we interviewed, most made the decision to abstain from any future use. However, those who did reduce their intake of alcohol and/or drugs generally developed and implemented strong personal rules limiting use. In a sense, these individuals taught themselves to use in a controlled fashion. For persons interested in decreasing problematic use of alcohol, see the websites for Moderation Management and Drink Wise identified in chapter 5.

Early-Phase Strategies for Natural Recovery

Overcoming addiction is a process that proceeds gradually. A person gains momentum, strength, and resilience as the time between dependence and recovery passes. It can be understood as a developmental process that is distinguished by an early stage and, later, a maintenance stage. Each of these stages is characterized by somewhat common yet unique challenges. In the remainder of this chapter we will identify strategies that appear to be particularly germane to the early phase of the self-recovery process. In the subsequent two chapters we will explore strategies associated with the maintenance and latter stages of natural recovery.

At the outset of your recovery effort, you need to make a decision about whether or not medically supervised detoxification is necessary. Many alcohol and drug users with long-standing habits gradually get clean by weaning themselves off these substances, while others, including many in our studies, quit abruptly. Though you may find that natural recovery is a viable option in your own case, a desire to pursue this course should not blind you to the potential dangers of acute withdrawal syndromes associated with certain chronic use of drugs, particularly alcohol and other central nervous system depressants such as barbiturates and benzodiazepines. Although withdrawal from dependence on stimulants like cocaine and opiates such as heroin can be extremely uncomfortable, this process is generally not dangerous or life threatening. On the other hand, however heavy cocaine and opiate users might be oblivious to their coexisting dependencies on alcohol and other depressants that can produce dangerous withdrawal effects.

In cases where there might be such dual dependencies, formal detoxification should be considered. Although such a process is clearly a form of treatment, medically supervised detoxification is of relatively short duration and generally takes three to seven days to fully complete. Many individuals complete detoxification and go on to productive lives free of drug and alcohol addictions without any further treatment or without attending support groups.

In addition to the discomfort of physical withdrawal, the early phase of recovery is often a fragile period. A range of emotional and physical uneasiness that can include, for example, ambivalence, loneliness, sadness, irritability, lethargy, and insomnia often characterize this stage. An effective response to these uncomfortable feelings requires you to take a proactive posture. It is also critically important to realize that such feelings are temporary and will pass. Unless there are chronic underlying physical or mental health problems, these feelings are normal and will generally diminish.

There are a number of strategies that self-remitters use to reduce the frequency, intensity, and duration of these uncomfortable feelings. Many useful strategies reported by natural resolvers include being active, engaging in physical exercise, partaking in soothing and invigorating nonexercise activities, modifying diets, and reducing or eliminating intake of common stimulants such as nicotine, caffeine, and sugar.

However, before you consider them as you begin your course of self-recovery, it is important to get a very thorough physical examination. Years of heavy substance use with the attendant problems of neglected diet, inactivity, and other poor health practices can put one at risk for an assortment of ailments and, in some cases, very serious diseases such has HIV, hepatitis, hypertension, and other conditions. Some of the strategies we recommend below and the benefits derived from them can have a profound impact on your physical health.

Being Active

During the early period of natural recovery you should strive to become active. Being active fills much of the void or emptiness felt in the early stages of recovery. When drinking and drug-taking activities are eliminated from the user's life and when social connections with users are terminated, a profound sense of emptiness is generally experienced that is further compounded by increased amounts of boredom and idle time. Being active will decrease pronounced thoughts about using during these idle periods and gives you a chance to engage in alternative activities that can reduce the boredom, loneliness, and other feelings that often lead to resumed use. The idea of being active does not suggest frenetic states of purposeless movement, but rather refers to participation in activities that encourage a physical and psychological invest-ment of time and energy that offers comfort and personal sat-isfaction. Examples of these kinds of activities might include taking a walk, gardening, bowling, hiking, house cleaning, and a variety of forms of moderate physical exercise. It is critical to understand the importance of "being active" as you start your journey of self-recovery so you can guard against the tendency to simply withdraw from the world through inactivity and reclusion. Such a passive approach would, in all likelihood, be counterproductive for most.

Physical Exercise

Physical exercise is, without a doubt, one of the best ways of being active. Because of the many benefits that are associated with physical exercise, in both the early and the latter phase of the recovery process, this activity warrants special atten-tion. The primary distinction between the type of physical exercise that we recommend for the early versus the latter phase of natural recovery is the level of intensity and dura-tion. During the early period of natural recovery, this level should be relatively moderate. The rationale is that during this time, particularly for the first few days, and perhaps weeks, persons with long-standing histories of addiction generally may not have the physical stamina or general state of health to undertake more rigorous exercise. People not in the habit of exercising on a regular basis can become easily discouraged with it if they push themselves too hard too early. Furthermore, they may be susceptible to painful or serious injuries if they are overly aggressive. Such injuries, of course, can prohibit some forms of exercise in the future.

During this early stage of natural recovery, consider short or relatively easy daily aerobic workouts that gradually increase in intensity and duration; for instance, go from 10 minutes to 20–30 minutes per session. Examples include walks, walk jogs, treadmill walking, moderate stairmaster walking, moderate bike riding, water aerobics, and a wide range of other low to moderate aerobic activities available at public recreation centers and gyms, YMCAs, health clubs, and fitness facilities accessible at most universities. These types of regular workouts hold enormous benefits at the outset of recovery. Many people trying to recover from addiction have reported that such activities reduce boredom and tension, improve sleep, and lead to an overall increase in health and sense of well-being. Regular moderate physical exercise can aid in your body's return to its normal health and accelerate the recovery process. As you begin to regain your health and increase your stamina, you will be able to increase the intensity and duration of workouts. This gradual increase further hastens the restoration of health and makes it easier to move to more rigorous workouts. However, before beginning a regular routine of any type of physical exercise, even the moderate workouts identified above, you should consult with a physician or a health-care professional. As stated earlier, years of heavy alcohol and/or drug use along with other hazardous behaviors might put you at risk for an assortment of mild to severe ailments, some of which could actually preclude certain forms of exercise.

Soothing and Invigorating Nonexercise Activities

Interviews with persons in our study and discussions with others who have defeated long-standing addiction without treatment report on the value of activities that are soothing and invigorating. They point out how activities such as getting a massage, taking warm and hot baths, steam baths, whirlpool baths, and sitting in saunas eases some of the physical and mental discomfort common in the early stages of quitting. While this kind of relief could benefit most of those struggling with the discomfort of the early phase of the recovery process, former heroin addicts report them to be particularly helpful. Cessation of habitual use of heroin and other opiates often results in mild to extreme body aches, frequently characterized as flulike symptoms. These soothing and invigorating activities, while rendering temporary relief from some of the discomfort, also allow the individual to experience, firsthand, the transitory nature of their unpleasant state. In many cases, such firsthand experience could be the difference between optimism about the possibility of truly feeling better and gloom about the expectancy of continued discomfort.

Quitting and Nutrition

During this early phase of natural recovery, you may need to come to terms with the consequences of many years of possible dietary neglect. Many alcohol and drug dependent persons have had very poor and often debilitating nutritional habits. The results of such negligence can exacerbate the already difficult task of recovery through diminution of health, increased discomfort, and decline in the body's ability to quickly return to a physical and mental state of normalcy. It is therefore crucially important that you begin, as soon as possible, to pay attention to your food intake in order to combat the deleterious effects of poor diet and begin the process of rebuilding health. The principle reason we emphasize this point is that the consequences of a poor diet not only impair the ability of the body to return to health, but consuming certain types of foods and beverages can actually aggravate the negative emotional and physical states common during this phase of the recovery process. These heightened adverse states can place one at risk for using again. Foods high in sugar and fats are good examples of foods that one should avoid during this period. Those who wish to make an especially informed effort to maximize the benefits of sound nutritional practices and minimize the negative effects of poor food choices should consult with a nutritionist, other food expert, or with some of the literature on nutrition currently available at health food stores, book stores, libraries, and on the Internet.

In fact, books are available that are exclusively devoted to exploring the relationship between nutrition and addiction. Some of these books offer a range of nutritional therapies and approaches to dependence on alcohol and various other drugs. Some of these books not only give suggestions for appropriate food choices such as whole foods, green leafy vegetables, and reduced fat, they also discuss supplementing food intake with various herbs, vitamins, and minerals during cessation efforts. Specific formulas for herbal teas, soups, salads, and other helpful recipes that can aid the recovery process are also presented in these books. Our review of these materials suggests, however, that it is best that you consult several sources, since some of these books present varying and sometimes opposing views about the same subject (e.g., contrasting views on the value of meats and dairy products). Approaching this literature in this way will allow you to discover common principles. These common themes are the ideas that you should seriously consider. We also caution that some of the earlier books tend to overly emphasize the biological explanation of substance dependence to the exclusion of the psychosocial explanations. Do not be overly concerned; take from these materials those ideas that make sense to you given our discussion in Part One of this book. Some of the books that you could consider include the following:

Spontaneous Healing, by Andrew Weil
Addictions: A Nutritional Approach to Recovery, by John Finnegan
How to Quit Drinking without AA, by Jerry Dorseman
Seven Weeks to Sobriety: The Proven Program to Fight Alcoholism through Nutrution, by Joan Larson

Beware of Common Stimulants

While several of the nutritional books identified above warn of the hazards of caffeine, sugar, and other common stimulants, we think that this issue warrants separate attention. We caution against the heavy use of beverages that contain large amounts of caffeine during the initial period of recovery. The rebounding effects of using excessive quantities of caffeine throughout the day can create a sense of mental and physical uneasiness that could put you at risk for resumed use of other more hazardous drugs. While intake of coffee is an obvious concern, drinking caffeinated soft drinks that have high levels of sugar can also prove quite troublesome. Excessive use of nicotine through smoking cigarettes or otherwise using tobacco products can also threaten one's success during this early period. We do not suggest that those who are nicotine dependent simultaneously quit their use of tobacco, at least during this initial period; that might prove to be too difficult. Because of the high potential for boredom and stress, we do caution against increasing the use of tobacco products and suggest that users stabilize their nicotine dependence at a reduced level. Both caffeine and nicotine use present unique challenges for drug and alcohol dependent persons beginning to undertake a course of recovery. While the up-and-down mood swings associated with use of these substances can compromise attempts to arrest dependency on other drugs, an abrupt break with caffeine and nicotine, with their own accompanying withdrawal syndromes, may profoundly worsen the negative experiences of the initial phase of recovery. It is important to note, however, that many persons who have overcome addictions on their own report they stopped smoking cigarettes and to a lesser degree, drinking coffee at the same time as they stopped using heroin, cocaine, and alcohol.

Take Action against Potential Insomnia

Perhaps one of the most troubling situations that accompanies quitting continuous use of intoxicating, stimulating, or, otherwise mind-altering drugs is insomnia. The restorative qualities as well as the overall health-related benefits of restful sleep are incalculable. Conversely, remaining awake or partially awake night after night to experience the physical and psychological anguish of withdrawal from some drugs can be tormenting. Many return to substance use, in some cases to different substances, because of their persisting insomnia or the anticipation of it. While most insomnia associated with discontinuation of substance dependency is usually temporary, we know of cases where persons claim to have experienced significant sleep disturbances for several weeks, and, in a few instances, several months.

Throughout this section of the book we emphasize the importance of improved health as a means for an improved sense of well-being and as a deterrent to using mind-altering substances. Of course, a major impediment for an improved state of health is lack of sleep and a vulnerability to poor health. We present the following ideas for combating insomnia and for an overall improved pattern of regular restful sleep. Some of these ideas were modified from suggestions for combating insomnia that are presented by Ray and Ksir in their book, *Drugs, Society, and Human Behavior* (8th edition).

First, determine how much sleep you need or think you need for maximum rest and restoration of your mental and physical functioning. If you have been using alcohol or other drugs heavily for long periods of time, you might have to guess at this or recall from earlier years. Though eight hours is the general rule, this standard does not apply to all; some need more and others do very well on less.

Establish a regular time that you go to bed and wake up to meet your optimal sleeping needs. Stick to those times, even on weekends and holidays, as best you can.

Be careful about what you eat in the evening hours and never eat heavy meals within 2 hours of going to bed. Small snacks can be okay, but avoid heavy loads on your digestive system as you near your sleep time. Conversely, annoying hunger may interfere with sleep. Be careful about intake of common stimulants like sugar and caffeine as you approach your sleep time.

Prepare a comfortable sleep environment. Persons generally sleep better in environments that are dark and slightly cooler than daytime temperatures or than warmer rooms. Conversely, rooms that are too cold can interfere with sleep. As best you can, avoid sleeping in environments where periodic loud noises or bright lights are likely to disturb you.

When you get into bed, turn off the lights and relax. Avoid attending to personal, work-related, or other kinds of problems while in bed. As best you can, only allow yourself to deal with these challenges during waking hours.

When there are numerous tasks for which you are responsible the next day or during the upcoming days, do not drudge over these matters in bed. Create a "things-to-do" list and give your attention to those concerns only during waking hours.

Exercise regularly but do not exercise vigorously near bedtime. Exercise can reduce some of the stress that occasionally interferes with sleep while simultaneously promoting sleep.

Do not lie awake in bed for long periods of time. If you cannot fall asleep within thirty minutes, get out of bed and do something relaxing; reading helps for some. Repeat if necessary. In these instances, an important consideration is to avoid developing a paired association between being in bed and restlessness. Avoid napping during the day. If an occasional nap is absolutely necessary, take only a twenty-minute nap. Extended naps can disturb the next night's sleep.

Avoid chronic use of sleeping pills. While pharmaceutical sleeping aids might be temporarily necessary under certain conditions, continuous use of these products generally does more harm than good.

Of course, some persons can experience chronic insomnia that is unrelated to their substance use or predates it. In such cases, we suggest formal assistance from health and mental health professionals who specialize in sleep disorders.

In the next chapter we turn our attention to strategies that can be useful in the later, maintenance phase of self-recovery.

CHAPTER 10

Maintaining Your
Recovery Naturally

The strategies that we have explored thus far are particularly relevant to the early phase of a recovery effort. We now turn our attention to more complex strategies that can help sustain a self-recovery effort. As with the discussion above, the strategies we identify here do not represent an exhaustive list, but rather consist of tactics we have learned from our studies on natural recovery. These strategies include changing environments, gaining social support, finding alternative forms of leisure and recreation, feeling good, engaging in meaningful work, assuming meaningful responsibility, experiencing conversions, and nurturing new identities.

Changing Environments

Changing their environment is a key tactic for many of those undertaking natural recovery, particularly those who are addicted to more illicit substances like cocaine and heroin. Even with the strong desire to change, continuous exposure to the cues and conditions under which use occurred could undermine recovery efforts. Visiting your same hangouts, interacting with the same friends with whom you used these substances, and continuing the same patterns of old activities represent the kinds of pressures that can inhibit recovery. Some who have employed natural recovery have talked about their need to permanently sever or at least temporarily cut off relationships with close friends and family members who contributed to their addictive use of alcohol and other drugs. Others left spouses who refused to quit or reduce their substance use. In some instances, people changed jobs or career paths altogether when their work environments exerted negative influences over their attempts to quit.

Moving or relocating to another city is a strategy that many self-remitters have employed. This "geographic cure," as it is commonly referred to by many in the addiction field, responds to the need for some addicted individuals to extricate themselves from the myriad of multiple and often intertwined circumstances that keep them mired in destructive substance use. Whether or not you choose to relocate physically is, of course, a decision that only you can make. However, even if you do not take such a drastic step, you should at least detach yourself from the drug scene.

Relationships

As most substance abuse researchers and longtime users know, addiction to alcohol and drugs emerges within a context of social relationships with others and, in most cases, is sustained by those relationships. While these relationships often play major roles in maintaining addiction, they also serve some of the same common needs that ordinary social relationships provide. The need for friendship, support, intimacy, acceptance, and a host of other social needs is realized through substance-using relationships. As these social networks are abandoned, it becomes necessary to cultivate meaningful relationships that do not reinforce heavy alcohol or drug use, but instead provide you with acceptance and support to help you through your personal transformation.

You can cultivate these supportive networks in various ways. Many of the self-remitters we have studied established new relationships with individuals and groups where alcohol or drug use were not central activities. Many others reestablished relationships with family members and friends who were not heavy substance users. Such relationships can be created or re-created in a wide variety of ways and settings. Many spoke of joining health clubs, choirs, church groups, and recreational sport teams as ways of meeting people. Some even contacted old friends or family members they had not seen in years as a way of helping them stay clean. Reconnecting with family members and old friends can be as rewarding for them as it is for you.

The workplace can also offer opportunities for establishing supportive relationships. Many workplace relationships can evolve into loving and nurturing ones that permeate beyond the walls of work. School is another setting where such relationships can evolve. A number of persons whom we have studied developed new relationships with people they met during their return to college or while enrolled in adult education courses. Others found supportive relationships in a variety of civic activities undertaken through choir groups, political groups, community groups, and religious groups. These are only a few examples of the wide range of opportunities that persons undertaking self-recovery can take advantage of to replace abandoned substance-using friends and groups. Whatever specific strategies you employ, it is important to remember that relying on the assistance and support of friends, family members, and acquaintances will not only help facilitate your natural recovery, but will also contribute to major improvements in your life more generally.

Leisure and Recreation

Heavy intoxicant use not only consumes a great deal of one's time and energy, but it can become an integral part of a person's pursuit of leisure and recreation as well. In fact, a life of addiction can be all-consuming. For many, when the addicted life is deserted so too are the primary means of obtaining thrills, excitement, and pleasure. Those addicted to substances for long periods of time have to find other channels of enjoyment and, for some, they actually have to learn how to have fun without alcohol or other drugs. For those who are completely immersed in the street subculture of illicit drug use, learning to enjoy life through conventional means can be particularly challenging. One heroin addict told one of the authors that he didn't know if he could stay clean because "straight people were boring." While the suggestions that we offer here may appear fairly simple and straightforward, former substance-dependent persons whom we have studied reported them to be of value as meaningful recreational outlets.

Joining various community clubs and groups can create opportunities to participate in numerous forms of pleasurable and fulfilling activities. Choirs, book groups, outdoor groups, hand drumming groups, and other community-based informal organizations can provide such opportunities. Team and league sports such as volleyball, softball, basketball, and team tennis provide similar opportunities. However, keep in mind that among certain team sports, beer consumption can be a central associated activity.

Persons attempting to overcome substance dependence can also find pleasure in individual sport activities that are simultaneously health promoting. Activities such as jogging, biking, swimming, racquetball, tennis, and the like have been found to be extremely beneficial. Similarly, health clubs and other fitness organizations offer a wide variety of enjoyable, health-promoting activities available in group as well as individual formats. Some of the group activities include, for example, aerobic, step-aerobic, jazzercise, rowing, and martial arts classes. At the individual level, a wide variety of workout equipment is available where persons can simulate jogging, rowing, biking, cross-country skiing, and a host of other enjoyable and invigorating activities.

Nighttime can be an especially challenging part of the day for someone who has constantly used alcohol and other types of drugs. Although for the heavily dependent person use might have occurred throughout the day, most use and social activities around use occur in evening hours. Many persons report that the void that is left when they quit is most apparent at night. We caution against too much movie watching or becoming overly engrossed with the Internet, particularly considering recent reports that persons often become isolated from family and friends because of their involvement with the Internet. Nevertheless, a good movie can be enormously entertaining, and there is almost no subject known to humankind that cannot be explored on the Internet.

Health and Fitness

Much of what has been discussed up to this point holds implications for improved health. Clearly, improving your state of health will go far in increasing your chances for success in accomplishing your goal of quitting or reducing your dependency on mind-altering substances. Improved health decreases the deleterious effects of years of physical neglect and leads to an increased sense of physical and mental well-being, which in turn negates much of the potential discomfort—feelings that often result in resumed use.

One of the principal reasons that persons addicted to alcohol and other drugs for long periods of time find it difficult to stay off these substances is that they often feel uncomfortable and sometimes outright miserable. Depending on the circumstances of use, this discomfort can range from mild to extreme. It can diminish appreciably over the course of a few days, or it can linger for several months with almost unnoticeable improvements. For example, persons who have been on high doses of methadone for extended periods and whose health has been significantly compromised through poor diet, inactivity, and other conditions report experiencing various levels of insomnia, body aches, restlessness, sadness, and an inability to focus for weeks and months after their last dose of the drug. They also complain about the "psychological discomfort" that seems to linger long after the physical discomfort subsides. Their experiences suggest that the feelings of emptiness, gloom, detachment, and similar conditions that characterize this state persist much longer than the physical uneasiness. Given these circumstances, it is not surprising that many return to using these substances within weeks and, in some cases, within days of completing treatment or making other attempts to stop.

Of course, the key to limiting the extent and duration of "feeling bad" is to increase your ability to "feel good" without necessarily using substances. A person's motivation to maintain a changed lifestyle will undoubtedly be compromised if he continues to feel poorly after weeks or months of abstinence or significant reduction. After all, as a former client of one of the authors asked, "Who wants to get clean to feel bad all the time"?

Again, paying attention to your health is an effective means by which you can reduce these negative sensations. For many, the level of health we recommend exceeds their pre-substance-use level, for others, getting healthy merely means a return to a state of health they enjoyed prior to their destructive use of alcohol and drugs. While many self-remitters become intensely involved in fitness types of activities, we are not suggesting that all such persons need to become preoccupied with health and fitness to feel better. There are multiple avenues to "feeling good" without using substances. Your task is to find what it is that gives you pleasure and provides you with intrinsic rewards that are no longer associated with substance abuse.

As stated earlier, regular physical activity and attention to nutrition can aid one's self-recovery effort in numerous and important ways. While the early phase of natural recovery should entail moderate workout regimes, in this maintenance phase of the recovery process you might consider moving to a more rigorous workout. Examples include jogging, lap swimming, long-distance biking, rowing, stair climbing, cross-country skiing, and group workouts such as aerobic, step aerobic, boxing aerobic, and spin-cycling classes. These kinds of workouts often result in heavy sweating and have been reported by many to have almost immediate effects on increased relaxation and their sense of well-being. Again, you should consult with a health-care professional before beginning a regime of physical exercise, particularly a more rigorous and strenuous one.

Persons overcoming long-standing alcohol and drug problems should also not ignore well-documented research as well as volumes of other more popular writings on the benefits of good nutrition. You cannot expect to experience noticeable improvements in health and the attendant benefits of improved physical and mental well-being on a poor diet of foods high in fats and sugars. One cannot consume large amounts of caffeine and smoke heavily and expect to enjoy an optimal level of health. While you do not need to become a "health zealot" to overcome alcohol and drug problems, you do need to be aware of the kinds foods that you consume and recognize that good nutrition can actually lead to noticeable states of improved physical and mental well-being.

At this stage in the recovery process, our discussion in chapter 9 also applies: if you have not already done so, consider augmenting your diet with vitamins, minerals, herbs, and other nutritional supplements. For example, silymarin, the active ingredient in the milk thistle plant, has been shown to be effective in reducing some of the harm caused to the liver by years of heavy use of alcohol and other drugs. Since the liver plays such a vital role in the body's processing of nutrients and in the elimination of toxins from the body, restoration of proper liver functioning alone can benefit one's health in an appreciable way. Also during this stage, and as discussed in chapter 9 about the early phase of recovery, consulting with a nutritionist, herbalist, or simply reading up on the subject of good nutrition can provide you with invaluable nutritional advice.

People who were formerly substance dependent but now enjoy markedly improved levels of health and sensations of feeling good are often amazed that they could experience this state without using mind-altering substances. In fact, one of the reasons reported by some for not returning to alcohol and drugs is that they do not want to jeopardize the physical and mental states that they enjoy and have become accustomed to. This, of course, does not suggest that good health is the panacea for drug addiction; however, those contemplating natural recovery need to be keenly aware of the fact that they can realize substantially improved health and fitness with only moderate effort.

Work

While involvement in work in the early stages of the recovery process can help fill some of the void that is often so pronounced during that time, continued employment in settings that are uninspiring can actually threaten your self-recovery effort. There is a large body of research and popular literature that underscores the importance of doing interesting, challenging, and gratifying work. The importance of engaging in satisfying work is particularly relevant to those who have long-standing histories of substance dependence and who are attempting to overcome such problems. Many of those we have we interviewed in our studies talked about the value of changing jobs and careers as they began their recovery journeys. Several reported returning to college to prepare for new careers. Others started their own businesses as they proceeded with their change processes. In most cases, these self-remitters threw themselves into these new pursuits with a passion.

While the people we interviewed were not representative of the total population of self-remitters, we feel strongly about the significance of meaningful work in sustaining recovery. Mundane, repetitive work routines with little or no intrinsic personal rewards can produce severe alienation, leading to a felt need to escape through the use of alcohol or other drugs. Also, such jobs typically do not provide the kinds of benefits such as health care, relative job security, and at least some limited flexibility that people need when making radical changes in their lives.

One of the appeals of working as a service provider in a drug and alcohol treatment program, for those who have had substance use problems, pertains to this principle. Even with the often-accompanying low wages, frustrating mounds of paperwork, and disappointing progress of many clients, this type of work can be very rewarding. The intense human contact, the excitement, and the sense of "making a difference" in this as well as other types of human service settings hold much appeal for many people. We are not suggesting that you necessarily seek employment in alcohol and drug treatment settings or in similar human service organizations. In fact, there can be some drawbacks to becoming an addiction counselor for those whose lives have been so intimately anchored to addiction and who have recovered without treatment. It would be difficult for many self-remitters to enter the drug treatment work given the emphasis of most programs on the disease explanations of addiction. However, this kind of human contact, along with the overall exciting climate inherent in a range of human service organizations, makes such work conditions particularly appealing for many former users.

Of course, there is a host of professional careers that offer similar opportunities: medicine, law, psychotherapy, and teaching, for example. These professions may be beyond the reach of many because of the professional-school entrance requirements as well as the amount of training required to practice. Nevertheless, there are many occupations that do not require this level of extensive training while still providing personal satisfaction. The key is to find employment that is nonalienating, intrinsically meaningful, and personally rewarding.

Finally, we realize that meaningful work can mean different kinds of work for different kinds of people, and that many people find work involving intense human contact totally unappealing. Obviously, other types of occupations should be explored by these individuals. We also realize that many persons, like some of those we have interviewed, in professional jobs in medicine and law find their work rewarding, yet they get into trouble with alcohol and drugs, or worse, develop such problems because of the stress of their work.

Ultimately, you need to carefully examine the work you do. Perhaps you are unhappy with it. For high-prestige professionals making large salaries, this can often be the case. Money does not necessarily bring about the happiness you may seek and may require making compromises that you find personally disconcerting. Inner satisfaction may be derived through jobs with lower amounts of stress and with greater intrinsic meaning. Since you may spend more than half of your waking hours at work during the week, you must take into account how your work conditions might affect your efforts to change.

Responsibility

Many people who have overcome substance addictions on their own have found that having family and work responsibilities as well as other serious obligations have tempered their urge to return to use. They have discovered that their new lives are something they value immensely and do not wish to threaten by resuming destructive habits. Assuming responsibility in your life can bring about healthy and rewarding changes. For instance, some drug-dependent women decide to get clean because of the birth of a child or because of pregnancy. Without question, the emerging responsibilities associated with being a parent can be uniquely rewarding. While unwelcome responsibilities can create unhealthy pressures that foster a need to escape, obligations to others can actually serve as a buffer against the return to use or at least to drug use that is destructive.

Careers, professional positions, and jobs that are highly valued can serve a similar purpose. Commitments to organizations and institutions beyond the workplace can also result in increased distaste for chronic substance use. Membership in churches, other religious organizations, community groups, civic groups, as well as participation in social and political movements can create forms of responsibility that many find gratifying. This is not to suggest that you should shoulder inordinate amounts of responsibility as part of your natural recovery strategy. Excessive responsibilities, particularly early on, could actually undermine your recovery effort. We are suggesting, however, that if you are attempting to terminate your destructive patterns of substance use, taking responsibility for your own actions as well as for meaningful activities that you truly cherish can go a long way in reaching your goal.

Belief

In one of our other books we explore the concept of conversion and its apparent role in the recovery process for many untreated as well as treated remitters. We will not attempt to give comprehensive attention to the concept here, but rather will present you an overview of its main characteristics as it relates to self-recovery. The conversion experience can be characterized as a fundamental departure from one's addicted life and its accompanying roles and behaviors to a focused immersion into an alternative, often radically different, lifestyle. We are not talking here about the conversion to an addict identity which is characteristic of many treatment programs. The kind of conversion that many of the self-remitters we have studied experienced was not to an addict identity, but, rather, to a new identity that was part of their natural communities.

For instance, many who have been substance dependent join religious groups where they become engaged in religious activities such as praying, reading the religious literature, attending church or temple services, and becoming personally active in other organized religious activities. Very often, these naturally occurring conversion experiences are all-encompassing and can promote many of the natural recovery strategies that we have discussed above. For example, it is well known that many African American males have resolved these kinds of problems by joining the Nation of Islam—the most well known case being that of Malcolm X. Those who join and remain loyal to the principles and teaching espoused by such a group create new social support networks, find new ways of leisure, modify their diets, assume meaningful responsibilities, and generally integrate into their lives much of what has been discussed above.

However, conversion experiences need not be religious in nature. For some, a complete immersion into the student role could mean that the former substance user who has become a college student now directs most of his or her energies toward activities that result in being an excellent student. The student attends all sessions of her classes; reads and studies all class assignments, including many of the suggested additional readings; develops an in-depth understanding of the content in her various courses; takes on leadership roles on campus; and through her devotion to learning, earns the respect of her fellow students and professors. While some might see this transformation as slightly extreme, as is the case with many who have observed conversions, the immersion into such newly found roles can serve to create a new set of values and opportunities that are totally inconsistent with heavy, chronic intoxicant use. Thus, you may not need to "convert" to an addict identity, but you may need to experience a natural conversion that allows you to develop a strong belief structure.

Identity

The majority of the self-remitters we have studied had abandoned their addict identities and had taken on more conventional roles. During our interviews with them, most took pride in telling us they did not see themselves as addicts. Instead, their identities centered on the various new roles they were performing, such as students, parents, and workers. Ultimately, those attempting to recover naturally from their addictions need to discover new selves and new ways of being that are deeply rewarding. Discovering "who you are" and becoming attached to social and community groups that support this emerging identity is perhaps the most important thing an individual can do to promote a self-recovery. In fact, people often discover "who they are" within the context of their life within established institutions and social relationships. People are much more than their addictions. All individuals are capable of accepting and expressing love, of offering and receiving community, and of creating meaningful social roles. Creating and nurturing new and more positive identities, while at times difficult, is almost always worth the effort.

Conclusion

The strategies we have discussed in this chapter are in no way intended to represent the only strategies that people who overcome addictions without treatment have at their disposal. The strategies are simply those that, in our view, were common among the self-remitters we have studied.

One of the things that struck us in the process of writing about people who have naturally resolved their addiction is that their experiences resemble what transpires in effective treatment and even in self-help groups. Although the approaches that we identified above are directed toward persons interested in self-recovery, they could also benefit those who are undergoing treatment, are in aftercare programs, or have completed treatment. In fact, most of this information would be especially useful to those who have completed an inpatient residential treatment program and are returning to their natural environments.

We also realize that persons may be reading this material who have had direct experience with or are otherwise knowledgeable about the pleasurable sensations that accompany the taking of these substances. Some might have reservations about the efficacy of some of our suggestions for the early and maintenance phases of recovery. Some might resist accepting the suggestion that improved nutrition and health can result in a state of well-being that counters the appeal of using these substances. Others might feel that simply severing relationships with using friends and creating new, healthier relationships would not necessarily prevent a return to destructive substance use. In a sense, they would be correct. No single suggestion alone will likely lead to successful self-recovery. It is only through a combination of these strategies that substance-dependent individuals are likely to realize fundamental changes in their addictive behaviors, and in their overall sense of physical and mental well-being.

Equally important is that the kinds of core changes that we have discussed generally occur only gradually, slowly becoming established routines in one's life. We have no optimal timeframe to propose, as each situation and each person is, of course, different. We know of successful cases where former alcohol and drug dependent persons realized a relatively comfortable, appealing, and stable state within a few months. We know of other self-recovery attempts that have wavered back and forth, including a return to problematic substance use, for several years before someone was finally able to enjoy a state of comfort and contentment that was independent of intoxicants. We also know of cases where self-recovery efforts have resulted in return to use, but at much lower and nondestructive levels that endured for many years. As discussed in other places of this book, controlled use or moderation after a period of chronic use does occur. But, like natural recovery, controlled use may be underestimated and of some benefit.

Finally, regardless of whether a person pursues self-recovery or enters treatment, we know that quitting alcohol and other drugs after many years of dependence is an arduous process for most. We are not oblivious to the sheer difficulty and torment that some experience in their genuine attempts to change their lives. However, among the self-remitters that we have studied, various combinations of these strategies did result in victories over the destructive dependent use of these substances by making their wearisome journeys less uncomfortable, more appealing, more meaningful, and more productive. And, because of their decision to quit alcohol and drug addiction on their own rather than by entering the established treatment system, their addict identities are mostly insignificant parts of who they were, rather than large parts of who they are.

◀ CHAPTER 11 ▶

Living without Addiction

After individuals have regained their health and rid themselves of most, if not all, of the remnants of physical and psychological discomfort associated with their former state of
substance dependence, how do they fully reintegrate themselves into a personally meaningful role within their existing
or new community? How do they successfully accomplish
this without allowing the past to assume a conspicuous role
of "shameful baggage" but rather serving as valuable insight
into how one negotiates extreme personal difficulty and becomes an improved person because of that experience? How
do they manage the challenge of abstinence in this latter
phase of cessation if they decide that is the most appropriate
course or how do they navigate the world of moderation or
controlled use if that is the direction you decide to take? This

chapter responds to these and several other important concerns that formerly substance dependent persons are likely to have when their relationship with mind-altering substances radically changes.

If you happen to have come this far in your journey already, we applaud your accomplishment and acknowledge that you have probably endured numerous difficulties to achieve this degree of transformation. Though your new relationship with alcohol and other drugs has probably eliminated several associated problems, you will still encounter the kind of day-to-day difficulties that ordinary people—those who have never been substance dependent—experience. While we do not subscribe to the view that substance dependence is a lifelong disease, having had this profound experience does hold implications for how you effectively interact with and negotiate your new world. For a time, at least, certain situations will require you to be more creative and vigilant than those who have not had your experiences. We conclude this section of the book by addressing the following important issues that you might want to consider as you reintegrate yourself into the normal world and supplant your old self with your new self:

- ► Current identity and the past identity
- ► Creating and maintaining new roles
- ► The reality of abstinence
- ► The Challenge of Moderation
- ► Maintaining a Sense of Well-Being

Current Identity and Past Identity

Think of this simple scenario. Sam returns home from a dinner party at a friend's home where there were fifteen other guests, mostly friends. Before going to bed, Sam realizes that his driver's license and American Express card are missing from his wallet, which was kept in his overcoat pocket. He frantically calls his friend and asks if she found his belongings. She thoroughly looks around her home but does not find these items. Both of them recall that Jimmy, a known former heroin addict, was at the dinner, and suspicions begin to mount about the likelihood that he lifted the driver's license and credit card from Sam's overcoat as it hung in the closet. Both surmise that he is probably in the process of changing the picture on the license so that he can charge on the credit card and may be opening a false checking account to begin a check-writing scheme. Sam immediately calls American Express to cancel his credit card and, out of anger, alerts several others who were at the dinner party to what he thinks happened to him. Several days latter, and to his surprise, Sam receives a call from his sister asking him to come pick up his driver's license and credit card that were left on her coffee table. She reminded him that he left these items after they opened a Sears account by phone to buy a refrigerator for their mother.

Those who undergo formal treatment and/or participate in 12-step groups are often exposed to recovery principles that suggest that they should have little reservations about sharing their past chronic use of alcohol and other drugs with others. Some propose that being forthright about this matter can actually be therapeutic. In many cases this could be true and we do not want to disregard any strategy that former addicted persons find helpful. However, one should not be so naïve to think that being a former "drug addict" or an "alcoholic" carries no social stigma. Most adults hold images of what drug addicts and alcoholics are, and such images, even among those who consider themselves open-minded, are generally far from endearing. In fact, many former addicts experience outright discrimination after such disclosure. Sam's scenario above speaks vividly about stereotyping, discrimination, and other drawbacks of being regarded an addict.

Consequently, we see no compelling reason why you should hold on to an identity of alcoholic or addict. In fact, most of what we have discussed thus far suggests that changing your life will necessarily require you to change how you regard yourself as well as how others see you in relation to your past identity. Indiscriminate announcements to others about your past difficulty can set the stage for the exact opposite: your attempts at change can unknowingly be undermined by others due to their expectations of what former addicts and, consequently, you are like. Though the old adage "once an addict always an addict" has no scientific basis, it is nonetheless a misconception held by many and one that can shape how others see you, trust you, value you, and hold expectations of you; and also how you regard yourself. In fact, many of the natural remitters we have studied over the years have not revealed their addiction to too many people.

Modifying the negative images that others may have of

you as a former substance abuser represents a different kind of identity management challenge. Some of these people may have been victims of your substance abuse and related behavior. You may have duped them in your schemes to raise money for drugs or otherwise taken inappropriate advantage of your relationships with them. In any case, you cannot simply say to them that you are no longer an alcoholic or drug addict—you must live it. Your deeds rather than your claims must speak to their reservations about you. And, of course, you do not demonstrate it by reminding them of your past behaviors; you allow your new life gradually to reflect and echo who you have become. In some instances, changing how some of these friends and relatives think of you can be an almost insurmountable challenge. Because of the intensity of some of the previous conflicts you may have had with these persons, some of wounds within these relationships will never fully heal.

As you can see, the overriding principle in this discussion is that your identity is shaped not only by what you think of yourself, it is greatly influenced by what others think of you as well. How they regard you is very much a reflection of what the larger society has conveyed to them around the permanency of addiction—a belief largely propagated by the treatment industry but unsubstantiated by science or even by basic common sense. This situation suggests that you really need to be thoughtful about whom you share these past experiences with. We are not suggesting that you hide important information about yourself from those very close you, such as prospective partners or spouses. That would be unfair to them. However, we do remind you that, unfortunately, there can be subtle and not-so-subtle prices to pay for this disclosure to others that you need to think about.

Creating and Maintaining New Networks

As discussed in chapters 9 and 10, one of the principal strategies used by persons in our studies to build new lives was to cultivate new friendships and become members of networks with people who were nonusers or nonproblematic users. In some instances, these new associations represented renewed friendships and relationships with family members as well as with former friends. As much of the substance abuse research, including our own, demonstrates, it is exceedingly difficult to extract yourself from the world of heavy alcohol and other drug use when you retain close ties with those who continue to live in it. There can be little argument against the wisdom found in the expression "we are who we associate with." In this latter, more stable phase of your change process, these new or renewed friendships are no less important than they were at the outset of your journey. The difference now is that instead of having to reach out to these persons, these relationships should be shaping into more reciprocal ones naturally. Your responsibility now is to nourish them, to ensure that they continue to provide you emotional and social comfort.

Taking care of these friendships will occasionally require some sacrifice on your part, and some of the activities that these friends and relatives want you to participate in may initially hold little appeal for you. This can be especially true when these activities are family events where "getting together" can feel more like a dreaded obligation than an opportunity for enjoyment. Be flexible here; this is not a one way street. Responsibility to family and friends to attend functions that you may not especially find appealing comes with being a member of a family or being a friend. Practice your listening skills. In conversations with these persons, become interested in them, in their opinions, and in things that interest them. Do not dominate conversations with your accomplishments, your agenda, and those things that only interest you. In this latter phase it is important to take care of these relationships because as you make the transition into your new life, in many ways these relationships are taking care of you.

The Reality of Abstinence in the Latter Stage

Most treatment programs and 12-step groups see abstinence as the only reasonable goal for someone who has been substance dependent. While we do not think that abstinence is the appropriate goal for all such persons, for those with extensive histories of chronic addiction who have failed at numerous attempts to cut back or have failed at treatment, we also think that abstinence is the most logical choice. In fact, because of the severity of their alcohol and drug dependencies, nearly all of the persons in our studies who had overcome these problems on their own reported that they practiced abstinence.

Before we proceed further, we need to clarify that while abstinence in this context is generally thought of avoiding all mind-altering substances, in reality that is often not the case. Many persons who claim to practice abstinence are concurrently addicted to nicotine and/or caffeine and have failed at numerous attempts to quit or cut back. While these addictions, particularly to tobacco products, can have be very destructive, many choose simply to live with the risks. However, there are many who have given up their cigarettes and cut back on coffee as they moved beyond the grip of substances like alcohol and cocaine, for example. The behaviors of these persons more accurately represent abstinence in its strictest sense.

Having clarified this important point, we can ask: What are some of the common challenges associated with abstinence maintenance that are likely to confront persons in this more stable phase of their transformations? In this section we will identify for you some of the issues we have discovered to be particularly germane to our clients and to persons who have participated in our studies. At the outset, we need to say that there are entire books written on abstinence strategies. Some have in their titles terms such as relapse prevention, staying clean, staying sober, and related titles that suggest their subject is abstinence maintenance. Most of the strategies these sources discuss focus on avoiding and dealing with what is referred to as "high risk situations," circumstances that increase the probability that use will occur even though one's goal is actually abstinence. Examples include avoiding socializing with persons with whom you formerly used, avoiding places where your use occurred, and learning techniques for coping with stressful situations. While some of these strategies continue to be relevant here, most are particularly essential during the earlier phases of a cessation effort. We hesitate to refer you to specific books because many that we have reviewed offer a rather simple genetic explanation of substance dependency to the exclusion of more comprehensive biopsychosocial explanations. However, if you have read Part One of this book, you should be able to sort through this material and take from it what is likely to be beneficial to you; there are some good ideas to be found in them if abstinence is your goal. While we will not attempt to cover all of the strategies found in these sources that pertain to this late phase, we can say that many of the specific strategies identified comport with those that we have discovered from our practice and research.

Although the difficulty of not using is different for different people, it is generally most pronounced in the earlier phases of quitting. Most self-remitters who were at a late stage of cessation told us that using just didn't hold the same appeal for them as it once did. And, unlike those using the "one day at a time" approach advocated by 12-step groups, these self-remitters tend not to struggle with urges and compulsions to use on a daily or even regular basis. Some of those we interviewed reported that they had not seriously contemplated using for many years. Persons at this stage may occasionally be tempted to use, but overall maintaining their abstinence is generally threatened in ways that can be somewhat different from earlier-stage risks. We can safely state that all situations that put those in the latter phase at risk are likely to threaten the abstinence of those in the earlier phase, but the inverse is not true. For example, abstinence for the more stable is generally not at risk on paydays or when they are bored, as could be the case with someone with less stability. Conversely, holidays such as Thanksgiving and Christmas were reported by several of our more stable study participants to precipitate thoughts about using. Of course, such holidays affect those in the earlier phases as well. Parties and celebrations where consuming alcohol is a central and expected activity can overwhelm those in the earlier phases. While they are generally not the same kind of threat for the more stable, they can produce uneasiness for some that are much further along. Major life crises tend to put persons at risk both in the earlier and latter stages of the quitting process. Unexpected crises such as deaths, spousal separations, loss of intimate relationships, and other misfortunes can threaten abstinence in those who stopped their substance use even years ago.

We want to conclude this section with two very important points. The first is to remember that if you are at this stage of transformation, there is a lot that you have accomplished, and much of this did not come easy. You have demonstrated an ability to endure physical discomfort, emotional anguish, and an overall state of struggling to get where you are. If you do happen to compromise your abstinence by giving in to an urge, all is not lost, and, given the tenacity that you have thus far demonstrated, you will probably bounce back from this brief "glitch" rather quickly. Although you may feel somewhat guilty about your indiscretion, you need not overreact by believing that you are back to "square one," that you might as well go back to the way you were years ago. That kind of self-limiting rhetoric has no scientific basis, and you need not buy into such thinking. You have accomplished much and, in all probability, you will accomplish much more.

The second point is that the whole idea of "relapse" (and you should note that we have not used the term until now) as it relates to substance abuse is a misnomer for many. Relapse is a term borrowed from medicine that generally implies that the user has violated his or her abstinence goal and is destined to return to an uncontrolled state of chronic, destructive substance use. While some former users do exactly that, there is no scientific evidence that concludes that after years of abstinence all, or even most, former users will return to this state. Again, as implied above, this belief is simply not supported by research. For many, "relapse" would not be a conceptually accurate term to describe a temporary setback. Words such as poor judgment, stumble, or a "bump in the road" would be more appropriate. These terms denote a temporary event rather than a permanent condition.

The Challenge of Moderation

Moderation or controlled use as an option for substance-dependent persons is a touchy subject among substance abuse treatment providers and for those who subscribe to the disease view of substance dependency. Some see the experience of substance dependence as a condition that permanently alters the mind to a disease state that makes the former user an addict for life. We disagree. While we recognize that all experiences, particularly powerful ones like drug use, intimate relationships, loss of loved ones, and other deeply intense encounters influence one's future behaviors, propensities, and beliefs, we do not subscribe to this pathology view. If such a proposition were actually true, for example, all caffeine and nicotine dependent persons would be doomed to a world of destructive addiction once they broke these habits. They could not drink alcohol socially or take medically prescribed mood-altering medications without succumbing to a life of dependence on these substances. While the pathology of the brain theory might apply to some former substance-dependent persons, this statement is simply untrue as a blanket statement that applies to all.

Although we concur with the view that abstinence is probably the safest goal, in writing this kind of book we cannot ignore the fact that it is not the only reasonable goal for all who have been substance dependent. Government-funded studies in the United States and Canada have concluded that many substance-dependent persons can reduce their use of alcohol as well as other drugs to more manageable, less hazardous levels. We caution you, however, that even leaders in the moderation movement agree that moderation would not be a sensible goal for many. In fact, just recently the founder of Moderation Management concluded that her addiction to alcohol was so severe that abstinence was the only reasonable goal for her. All severely addicted persons are likely to be poor candidates for a moderation strategy. Conversely, those with less extreme dependencies, with no previous contact with treatment, and those from stable family, work, and community environments are better candidates for this approach.

Those who choose moderation may want to consider several key points that we think are instructive. First, make no grand pronouncements that you are going to cut back. Simply make plans to do so and set a date for implementing that plan; then do it. Your plan should include a beginning period of abstinence from your drug of choice and from other powerful mind-altering drugs. Moderation Management sets a time frame of at least thirty days of initial abstinence before attempting to reduce use of alcohol. We think that the longer the better, and suggest two months or ten weeks. If you are nicotine dependent, you don't need to quit using tobacco now, but, as discussed earlier, do not increase use during this abstinence period. If you can, cut back. If you drink coffee or otherwise use caffeine, you need not stop your caffeine use altogether, but it would be wise to reduce it and, if possible, limit your intake to morning and afternoon hours. If you can drink coffee late into the evening hours or immediately before going to bed and still fall asleep easily, there is a good chance that you have developed and continue to maintain a high tolerance for coffee. While this is not seen as a problem in our society, be aware that technically speaking you are still substance dependent. Unless you plan on maintaining this addiction, it will eventually pose problems for you as you attempt to manage your primary substance dependence, so now is a good time to cut back. It is important to point out again that many formerly substance dependent persons actually suspend their cigarette smoking and coffee drinking altogether as they resolve their primary addictions.

A number of people switch from one substance to another as a way of reducing out-of-control daily use. In fact, because of the legal status of alcohol and its similar pharmacological properties, it is widely known that many heroin users often quit heroin altogether and begin using alcohol exclusively. For some, this can be a useful strategy to reduce use; for others, it simply means substituting dependence on one substance for another, and it turns out to be equally disastrous. Because the cumulative effects of each of these drugs are different, one cannot use them in the same way and manage their desired impact. Easy and legal access to alcohol further compounds this problem since few societal restrictions are in place to prevent people from overconsuming. Because people use their "drugs of choice to get high," rather than to socialize, they generally have not learned to use alcohol socially. This does not mean that they can't; it means that before they can, they must change the purpose of their use. If that purpose cannot be changed or radically modified, they will find social use of alcohol, in particular, difficult. In our practice and research, we have discovered very sophisticated drug users who have switched drugs and managed one considerably better than the other. However, such persons generally have very strict self-imposed rules about amount and frequency, and under what conditions use occurs.

In chapter 5 we introduced you to several new organizations that specialize in helping those interested in moderation and in other alternatives to traditional treatment. Among other services, those organizations can help you determine whether or not moderation is an appropriate goal for you. They will also provide you with guidance about how to best to accomplish that goal if you are an appropriate candidate. They provide this help through books, reading materials, assistance via the Internet, and through a host of other methods and formats. Some even offer a face-to-face consultation, where a moderation specialist, including licensed clinical psychologists, will come to you just about anywhere. Before you set out on the path of moderation, we strongly encourage you to consult these sources. While you can purchase certain reading materials and specific services from these organizations, much of what they have to offer is free. You can even attend online meetings with some of these groups. Be aware, however, that most of these organizations advocate moderation as a goal only for those dependent on alcohol. To do otherwise could pose a slight ethical dilemma for them, since use of most other popular drugs is illegal, except under the guidance of health-care professionals. However, the programs of these organizations could also have some relevance for those dependent on street drugs and other illicit substances.

Finally, it is important to note that some of those we studied told us that they had attempted moderation with alcohol and that they achieved it, but then chose abstinence instead. One of the reasons given was that paying attention to the quantity and frequency of their drinking was too much of an imposition on them. Others' comments suggest that they formerly drank to achieve a certain "buzz" or a specific pleasant state of consciousness, and that moderation did not permit you to "get all the way there." In short, some of those who had either tried moderation or considered it felt that it was not worth the trouble. Many others felt they simply could not control their use or that the risk associated with failure in their particular case was too great.

Maintaining a Sense of Well-Being

Many have experienced life in the world of substance abuse as one characterized by mayhem, continuous crises, and other chaotic conditions. While this kind of chaos generally creates a host of problems for these persons, in their new lives they often miss the chaos or, as some studies characterize it, the excitement. This is particularly apparent as one begins the earlier phase of quitting. Persons often report difficulty with boredom and have told us that the key to their success during this period was staying active. For most, during the middle period this need begins to dissipate and as persons begin to settle into the latter phase the necessity for regular activity can noticeably diminish. Not all people will need such stimulation, but they may still at least occasionally feel a void or sense of emptiness even during the latter stages of their transformation. Although there is some inherent comfort in knowing that you are "clean" or have otherwise managed your former addiction, this satisfaction does not mean that joy, contentment, and a continuous sense of well-being will automatically follow. We know, and assume you also know, that many people without substance abuse problems also lead miserable lives.

In order to truly move beyond simply being sober or merely living without problems with substance abuse, you will have to make a deliberate effort to increase the quality of your existence. And, as most of us know, such knowledge and skills do not come naturally or simply with having quit or reduced one's substance use. You will need to acquire these competencies. Then you, and you alone, will need to act. Others can point you to sources of information, or otherwise be supportive of your efforts to improve other aspects of your life, but it will be up to you to take action and make sure that those changes become an integral part of your life.

Successful self-recovery after extensive periods of chronic use is very much related to regaining and maintaining one's health. During the latter phase of the quitting process, the importance of good health might not be as apparent but it is no less important. We hope that by now some of the points we made about the role of regular exercise and improved diet have actually become the norm for you. Although some of the people we interviewed in our studies became consumed with their health, you need not become a health fanatic to reap the benefits of an improved lifestyle. Barring unknown health or mental conditions, you will find that there is a direct relationship between improved health and an improved sense of well-being. We have interviewed former users who, after regaining their health, reported to us that they never imagined that they could feel so good without alcohol or without using other drugs. As already mentioned, several practiced abstinence because they did not want to jeopardize their new state of well-being. We see health as playing a critical role in maintaining the gains that former substance-dependent persons have made in their efforts to permanently move beyond substance dependency. Their health will have a major influence on the quality of their post-addict lives by serving either as a protective factor against resumed destructive use or, conversely, by making them vulnerable to such use.

Attempting an overhaul of the quality of life is, of course, an effort that would benefit most people in modern society, not just formerly substance dependent persons. Many people are stuck in ruts of one kind or another and have just not taken the time to self-reflect about their circumstances and/or contemplate ways of getting unstuck. Even if you see no other benefits resulting from your former lifestyle, there is at least one: you have been forced to self-reflect and to make changes. And, while not all changes result in personal growth, no personal growth can occur without some degree of change. So, in a way, your crisis is actually an opportunity that many others never have—some whose life problems are equal to or greater than yours. The comments of the Dalai Lama are instructive in this regard:

It is worth remembering that the time of greatest pain in terms of wisdom and inner strength is often that of greatest difficulty. . . . Unfortunate events, though potentially a source of anger and despair, have equal potential to be a source of spiritual growth.

However, in order to take full advantage of this opportunity and truly make improvements in these broader areas, you will need to begin to act on your commitment to do so by first seeking guidance or assistance.

Some of that assistance can come from professionals such as clinical social workers and psychologists who are skilled in helping people improve the overall quality of their lives. Many of these professionals provide this help in the form of counseling or psychotherapy and refer to it as providing assistance in areas of self-fulfillment, finding meaning, and self-actualization, for example. There are, however, numerous less formal, less expensive resources available to help you with self-improvement. One of the first places to start is your local bookstore. Local libraries also carry a number of books and magazines that focus on self-improvement. You can search various on-line bookstores like www.amazon.com and www.barnesandnoble.com for such books as well. Inspiration books by the Dalai Lama, Thomas Merton, and Deepak Chopra have helped many people find a sense of meaning in their lives.

One of the best sources for self-improvement material that focuses on the broader areas of your life and one that we mention when we give talks around the country on addiction recovery is in the form of audio cassette tapes, compact disks, videotapes, and computer software. These presentations cover a range of topics directed at personal self-improvement. Many of the ideas of some of the more popular books on self-improvement can be found in these formats. There are several companies that create and sell these materials, but the company that we have used over the years is Nightingale-Conant Corporation, on the Web at www.nightingale.com. We have been very impressed with the range of topics that their materials cover and have been especially pleased with their return policy. If you are not satisfied with the tapes, the CDs, the videos, or the software you order, you can return them within thirty days and will be given a full refund. While many people listen to the tapes and CDs in their homes, many others listen to them in their cars when traveling back and forth to work; this is an easy and more efficient way to listen to them.

Regardless of the source or sources you use for improving the overall quality of your life, our studies suggest that simply arresting your substance abuse problem is not enough by itself to make your life more meaningful; it is only the beginning. Your challenge now is how to meet this formidable task, one that is unfamiliar to most in the general public.

In summary, we remind you again that if you are entering this stage of the transformational process you already deserve lots of praise for your accomplishments. And, while you have accomplished much, there is still much ahead that you will have to attend to as you move toward a more complete and fulfilling existence. Although the part of the path that you now travel may be less tumultuous than it was earlier, your journey is just beginning. We hope that the suggestions we have provided in this book will take you far into that journey, one that is wonderfully exciting, deeply rewarding, and free from drug problems.

William Cloud is Associate Professor at the Graduate School of Social Work at the University of Denver, where he developed and has been chair of the Drug Dependency Concentration in the M.S.W. program.

Robert Granfield is Associate Professor of Sociology at the University of Denver. His primary interests lie in the areas of drugs and society and the sociology of law. He was formerly a director of an alcohol and drug abuse program for adolescents outside Boston.

Together, Cloud and Granfield are the co-authors of *Coming Clean: Overcoming Addiction without Treatment* and have taught, conducted research, and worked in the field of addiction for over twenty-five years.